Retaining Your
Best People

The Results-Driven Manager Series

The Results-Driven Manager series collects timely articles from *Harvard Management Update, Harvard Management Communication Letter,* and the *Balanced Scorecard Report* to help senior to middle managers sharpen their skills, increase their effectiveness, and gain a competitive edge. Presented in a concise, accessible format to save managers valuable time, these books offer authoritative insights and techniques for improving job performance and achieving immediate results.

Other books in the series:

Teams That Click

Presentations That Persuade and Motivate

Face-to-Face Communications for Clarity and Impact

Winning Negotiations That Preserve Relationships

Managing Yourself for the Career You Want

Getting People on Board

Taking Control of Your Time

Dealing with Difficult People

Managing Change to Reduce Resistance

Motivating People for Improved Performance

Hiring Smart for Competitive Advantage

Becoming an Effective Leader

Business Etiquette for the New Workplace

A Timesaving Guide

THE RESULTS-DRIVEN MANAGER

Retaining Your Best People

• • •

Harvard Business School Press

Boston, Massachusetts

Library of Congress Cataloging-in-Publication Data

Retaining your best people.
     p. cm. — (The results-driven manager series)
     ISBN 1-59139-973-4
     1. Employee retention. 2. Personnel management. 3. Labor turnover.
     I. Harvard Business School Press. II. Series.
     HF5549.5.R58R485 2006
     658.3—dc22

                                                              2005018859

Contents

Contents

Contents

Introduction

• • •

How much turnover is your team or unit experiencing? Do you tend to keep your most valuable employees, or lose them to rival companies? In an age when the job market swings cyclically toward and away from job seekers' advantage, much of the responsibility for retaining top-shelf talent during labor shortages rests with individual managers such as you. Indeed, during drum-tight labor markets, many organizations tie managers' variable compensation to retention rates, as well as reward managers who help valued employees find other jobs within the company rather than with rival firms.

Why are more companies emphasizing the importance of retention as a core competitive strategy? We're living in the knowledge era, and a company's human capital constitutes its most crucial competitive edge. But demographic changes point to an impending labor shortage of unprecedented magnitude. According to a 2000 Bureau of Labor Statistics report, by 2010 there could be as many as 10 million more jobs available in the United States than there are employees.

By keeping and engaging more of your best employees, you may benefit handsomely in financial terms if your company rewards retention with bonuses and other monetary incentives. You'll also generate enormous value for your organization. Teams that boast loyal, talented, and enthusiastic members:

- Inspire the loyalty and commitment of other employees

- Provide better customer service because they've acquired deep knowledge of their company and its customers

- Engage in more creative, collaborative thinking

- Find great satisfaction and meaning in their work

- Forge powerful bonds among members—connections that deepen their loyalty even further.

With these kinds of results at stake, what manager can afford *not* to improve retention in his or her group?

A Complex Strategy

Though most managers understand the importance of retention, too many step up their efforts to retain valued employees only when the labor pool is shrinking. Not unreasonably, that approach strikes employees as only self-serving. Instead, take a long-term view of retention. Specifically, what kind of culture will you craft to convince your best employees that it's worth staying with the company—even when times are tight and monetary rewards slim? How will you manage and motivate your people so as to win their loyalty to your team and organization? How will you communicate your appreciation of your best performers, as well as persuade them to feel personally responsible for their work?

All this requires a complex blend of Grade A people-management skills—ranging from creating a work environment that allows for flexibility, growth, and development to getting your best people more deeply engaged and thus more committed to your organization. But that's just the beginning. To keep and engage more of your talented staffers, you also need to know how to take advantage of techniques such as performance reviews, coaching, and incentives to improve retention.

Yet in the retention-strategy game, one size doesn't fit all. That's because different types of employees—managers, women, "50-somethings," young workers—have different needs and are motivated by markedly different interests while making career choices. Each group also offers its own unique forms of value. For example, younger workers bring fresh perspectives to the table, while more seasoned employees bring deep knowledge of the industry in which your company operates. To capture this value and engage each of these groups, the savviest managers customize their retention strategies accordingly.

Finally, merely hanging on to talented direct reports isn't enough. You also need to extract maximum value from these individuals. When people see that they're contributing to their organization's success, they feel more committed to their jobs. Extracting value includes getting the best from your employees as well as capturing their knowledge. That way, if they *do* ultimately move on to other groups in the company or another organization all together, your team or unit will still be able to put that knowledge to work. Extracting value also means eliciting the most innovative ideas from workers, as well as helping them to feel deeply engaged in their work. Engaged employees provide better service—creating engaged customers, who in turn spur your company's growth, profitability, and stock price.

If you've concluded that retention is far more complicated than you originally assumed, you're right. But that doesn't mean it can't be mastered. The articles in this volume provide a wealth of valuable guidelines. Here's a preview of what you'll find in these selections.

Making Retention a Core Strategy

The most effective managers demonstrate specific retention-related skills—such as the ability to attract talented employees to their organization, awareness of the early warning signs of defection, and provision of opportunities that enable valued employees to advance their careers. The articles in this section survey the broad range of skills you'll need to improve retention in your group.

Business editor Paul Michelman opens the section with "Why Retention Should Become a Core Strategy Now." According to Michelman, many workers prefer to stay with their current employer if their manager presents them with opportunities to grow, develop their skills, and position themselves to move forward in their careers. How to provide those opportunities? Learn as much as you can about your employees. Ask questions such as, "What can we do to keep you? What kinds of things do you want next in your career?" Also, let your best people know that you treasure them, count on them, and want to reward them in as many ways as possible. The payoff? They'll be more likely to hang in there with you, even when "talent poachers" come sniffing around.

In "Aligning Human Capital with Business Strategy: Perspectives from Thought Leaders," management consultant Cassandra Frangos surveys three experts' thinking about retention and strategic management of employees. For example, Dr. Jack Fitz-enz (author of *The ROI of Human Capital* and founder and chairman of the Saratoga Institute) urges managers to familiarize themselves with metrics related to retention (such as cost of turnover) and strive to meet aggressive targets (for instance, "25 percent reduction in turnover by year's end").

In this same article, David Norton (co-creator of the Balanced Scorecard performance-management methodology and co-founder of the Balanced Scorecard Collaborative) maintains that by objectively measuring talented employees' contribution to a company's strategy, managers can better manage their human assets. Together with their human resources executives, managers must develop a standardized set of measures and benchmarks—as well as a common language—for sharing knowledge about the strategic value created by the company's workforce.

The third expert in this article—Helen Drinan, former CEO at the Society for Human Resource Management—advises managers to deepen their understanding of the macro business environment in which their company operates, as well as the long-term workforce challenges coming down the pike. Only then can managers build successful retention strategies.

The next article, "Employee Retention: What Managers Can Do," describes a rich array of retention practices, including ways to recognize early warning signs of defection. (Symptoms include a change in behavior, such as coming in later than usual; a decline in performance; and references to "burnout.") The article also provides a "managing for retention" checklist. For instance, to "create a great environment," take a genuine interest in them as individuals. Freely dispense information about the business and its strategies—you'll show that you trust your people with the data and respect their ability to support the company's objectives. To "create great jobs," give people assignments that stretch their skills. And to spot—and address—dissatisfaction early, get regular feedback from employees on the work environment and your management style. Sidebars in this article provide further information on helping change-hungry employees to find new opportunities within the company, as well as crafting job offers that attract people who will fit best with your company—and therefore be most likely to stay.

You'll find additional valuable suggestions in "How to Keep Your Company's Star Employees." Author Edward Prewitt confirms a fact that many managers find startling: Pay is the least important motivator of an employee's loyalty to his or her organization. Indeed, an overemphasis on pay can prove corrosive to a company—because it encourages employees to jump to the next organization that offers them a bigger salary. Rather than throwing money at star performers to keep them, craft the right work environment. That includes offering valued employees plenty of opportunities to learn new skills and providing constructive feedback on their performance. Moreover, given that a "bad boss" is one of the most common reasons for the departure of top-performing workers, ensure that you treat your direct reports right.

In this section's final article, "Do People Want to Work for You?" business writer Loren Gary takes a closer look at the impact of skillful management on retention. The author lays out five fundamental competencies required to enhance your reputation as a "manager of choice." For example, retention starts with *talent scouting*: To get the best talent in the right places, ensure that candidates' "total job-shopping experience stands out from that of other talent competitors." That means participating actively in the selection and hiring process, rather than "outsourcing" it to the human resources department.

Additional competencies include *relationship building* (assimilating new hires into your group's culture) and *trust building* (demonstrating your credibility, taking pride in your employees, treating them with respect and fairness, and fostering a sense of team identity). Gary also emphasizes *skill building* (enabling employees to continually polish their existing abilities and acquire new ones) and *organization brand building* (enhancing your company's image in the minds of your direct reports).

Engaging Your Workers

The articles in this section closely examine several particularly potent techniques for engaging your workers. The advantage of boosting the engagement level of high-performing workers? You strengthen their commitment to your company.

In "Whose Job Is Employee Satisfaction?" business editor Angelia Herrin shines the spotlight on performance reviews. According to Herrin, too many managers use performance reviews only to set expectations and goals. Yet these meetings offer valuable opportunities for managers to engage top performers in their work—by praising good performance and listening closely to their employees' concerns. Use review sessions to discuss what workers want and need, and you can nip dissatisfaction in the bud and turn thoughts of defection into feelings of loyalty.

One key: Encourage employees to be as specific as possible about the sources of their dissatisfaction. If a worker asks for more money, be aware that such requests more often represent a hunger for appreciation, dignity, and respect. In such cases, invite the employee to make a list of what appreciation would look like on the job. And don't forget to review the available resources—such as training programs or stretch assignments—that can help satisfy employees' desire for professional development.

Paul Michelman, author of "How Great Managers Manage People" (the next article in this section), explores employee engagement further. Thanks to the continuity that engaged employees' longer tenure creates, these workers provide better service to customers—increasing the latter's engagement as well. Customer engagement in turn drives your company's growth, long-term profitability, and stock price.

Michelman describes several approaches to enhancing employees' engagement. One tactic entails seeking and rewarding employees whose talents redefine how a particular job is done. For example, customer-service representatives who use the telephone as a tool of intimacy manage each customer relationship more effectively than those who lack this talent. Another technique is to help direct reports build on their existing unique strengths—to take advantage of what they already do well.

Coaching can also serve as a powerful tool for engaging valued employees. Business and marketing writer Martha Craumer turns to this subject in "How to Coach Your Employees." Why does skillful coaching improve retention? It's an interactive process through which you help your employees define and achieve their professional aspirations. And workers who achieve their career goals are more likely to stay with their employer.

Like other managerial responsibilities, coaching requires specific skills. For instance, during coaching sessions, you need to focus all of your attention on your employee, listen actively to his or her concerns and viewpoints, and ask open questions (those that don't require a "yes" or "no" response) to encourage the person to explore new options and see things from fresh perspectives. Craumer outlines additional skills essential to coaching and explains how to build and leverage mutual trust and respect through the coaching relationship.

How you recognize and reward good performance can also strongly influence your ability to engage talented workers. Why? Recognition from a talented employee's manager makes him or her feel special—thereby fostering loyalty and commitment to the person's team and company. In "Employee Recognition and Reward," business author and employee motivation expert Bob Nelson offers tips for delivering effective recognition.

For example, the sooner you acknowledge good performance, the more clearly you send the message that you value that employee—and the more likely he or she will be to repeat the desired performance. Selecting the right kind of praise also matters. Find out what forms of recognition your people prefer—such as a handwritten thank-you note, an e-mail expressing your appreciation, a personal visit from you, or a public announcement of the person's achievement during a team or department meeting. During tough economic times, when monetary rewards dry up, a word of support and appreciation or a team lunch to celebrate a success can still go a very long way—and cost little.

Business professor Alan Randolph concludes this section with "Real Empowerment? Manage the Boundaries," which focuses on strategies for deepening employees' sense of ownership over their work. The more responsibility your people feel for their jobs, the greater their commitment to your company.

According to Randolph, your savvy use of boundaries—definitions of what your people are expected to do—can deepen your employees' feelings of ownership. For example, by gradually increasing the complexity of your employees' responsibilities, you foster a sense of mastery. In one manufacturing company, shop-floor teams initially were allowed to make decisions about simple tasks, such as measuring quality. As they gained experience, they took on more complex tasks, such as selecting work methods. Their motivation and performance soared.

Another boundary-management strategy involves praising progress and widening boundaries as soon as you sense discouragement setting in. Managers at one utility company addressed discouragement by asking employees to define and work toward performance-improvement goals for their team. The initial trickle of ideas soon turned into a flood, including a suggestion regarding parts salvage that saved more than $100,000.

Customizing Techniques to Employee Types

Different groups of employees—managers, women, older workers, younger workers—have unique forms of value to offer and distinctive interests that they weigh while making career choices. To capture their value and win the loyalty of the best among these groups, adapt your retention and engagement strategies accordingly.

The first article in this section is "Keys to Retaining Your Best Managers in a Tight Job Market," by business writer Marie Gendron. According to Gendron, companies are finding it harder than ever to hold on to their talented managers. Your strategies for fighting back include identifying roles in which pay is a big issue—often management positions in information technology. In such cases, take steps to provide competitive salaries, which you can determine by tracking classified ads, networking with members of human resources organizations, and asking trade organizations. In roles in which salary is not a large concern or payroll is tight, consider increasing managers' participation in equity. Also watch for and address signs of burnout—a cause of defection that's particularly common among overburdened managers.

Business writer Kristen Donahue addresses retention of valued female employees in this section's next article, "Why Women Leave—And What Corporations Can Do About It." As Donahue explains, many talented women depart companies to start their own entrepreneurial ventures because they encounter obstacles to advancement in the corporate realm. The resulting "brain drain" hurts companies.

How to reverse the drain? Facilitate discussion and exploration of gender-equity issues. Ask whether you need to work harder to ensure that women are included in important business interactions—such as informal business networking, mentoring relationships, and after-hours socializing with clients. Also strive to eradicate "invisible" barriers to women's success, such as damaging stereotypes about female employees that influence decisions about who gets promoted and who wins career-advancing project assignments. In addition, promote understanding of the unique value that women bring to the table—for instance, a greater tendency to encourage information sharing and use a more open management style.

"How to Keep Your 50-Somethings" shifts this section's focus to retention of seasoned workers—the baby boomers who have earned a reputation for reliability and productivity, and who possess most of your company's intellectual capital. With massive retirements impending among this employee population, you need to develop plans for keeping these valuable individuals and leveraging their value.

Customized compensation plans can help; for example, enabling larger contributions to retirement funds. Many older workers also greatly appreciate flexible hours as well as the opportunity to work part-time, share jobs, and telecommute. Autonomy—being able to work on their own and explore intriguing new challenges—can further "sweeten the pot" for older workers who are considering whether to stay with their current employer. Merely opening a dialogue with 50-somethings—asking how their needs are changing and what would constitute the ideal employment situation—can uncover fruitful avenues for exploration.

"Finding—and Keeping—Good Young Employees" explores the other end of the age spectrum. Owing to tight labor markets and a remarkably small post-baby-boom age cohort, the number of workers aged 25 to 34 has declined about 12 percent since 1990—and is expected to continue dropping. These trends prevent organizations from leveraging the fresh perspectives that young people bring to the workplace.

To address this concern, blend recruitment, retention, and reorganization strategies. For example, develop "value propositions" differentiating your company from rivals in the minds of young job candidates. To keep young people loyal, consider providing unusual benefits that they value—such as auto insurance, home insurance, and prepaid legal services—in addition to health coverage. Finally, design fluid jobs that appeal to young workers who take a free-agent, entrepreneurial approach to work. For instance, let them take sabbaticals, consulting deals, or on-again-off-again assignments if such arrangements interest them and serve your company's needs.

Extracting Maximum Value from Employees

It's not enough to merely hang on to talented workers; you also need to seize advantage of the unique knowledge, ideas, and skills they bring to your workplace. When people see their talents being put to use in their organization, they feel appreciated. That in turn engenders commitment to the organization.

Business writer Alan G. Robinson offers recommendations for extracting value from top performers in "Getting the Best Employee Ideas." The author emphasizes the importance of getting employees' "small ideas"—notions that may seem minor on their own but that collectively improve your organization's performance. Unlike big ideas, maintains Robinson, small ideas aren't visible to your company's rivals. Thus they can't be countered or copied as easily. For this reason, small ideas give your firm a competitive edge. Employees generate more small ideas when they discover that their previous suggestions have been embraced and used. So implement good ideas rapidly and give prompt credit to the employees who provided them.

The next article in this section—consultant Melissa Raffoni's "Honing Strengths or Shoring Up Weaknesses: Which Is More Effective?"—explores the importance of exploiting high performers' unique abilities. To extract maximum value from your top performers—and thereby boost your chances of retaining them—Raffoni recommends that you balance building on employees' strengths with addressing their weak areas. Why? Ensuring that your company's needs are met often requires both.

Strategies for improving weak areas include emphasizing the strategic importance of shoring up a particular problem area. Describe the cost, to the employee, of neglecting that ability. And make the skills-strengthening process as painless as possible. For instance, suppose an employee struggles with time management—but you know that he also finds technology fascinating. In this case, you could give him access to time-management tools that would help him as well as capture his imagination.

When you're managing change-hungry performers who may eventually move to other groups in your organization, extracting their value becomes especially imperative. To be sure, keeping them within your company is far better than losing them to a rival organization. Yet in moving elsewhere in your organization, these individuals may take important knowledge with them that your team needs in order to excel.

Consultants David Boath and David Smith of Accenture address this concern in the section's final article: "When Your Best People Leave, Will Their Knowledge Leave, Too?" These authors present strategies for capturing knowledge residing in your most productive staffers. For example, identify where you're most at risk from the loss of information and experience. Which individuals, if they departed your group, would leave a major vacuum? Establish a succession-planning program for ensuring that important vacancies are filled with equally valuable players. And use technology—such as e-learning and performance simulation techniques—to capture experts' insights and build a learning community around them.

Holding on to your best people requires a complex blend of managerial skills. As you read the selections in this volume, keep the following questions in mind:

- Which employees in your group would you most regret losing?

- How can you best demonstrate your appreciation of those individuals?

- What actions might you take to craft a work environment that will secure these employees' commitment to your team and your company?

- What do your best people want from their professional lives? Is it opportunities to advance their careers? A chance to work with people they like? Variety in their work assignments? How might you discover and fulfill these needs— thereby winning your people's loyalty?

Make Retention a Core Strategy

• • •

To make retention and engagement of your employees a core competitive strategy, you need to sharpen specific skills. These include knowing how to attract talented individuals to your organization, recognizing early warning signs that valued employees may be thinking about leaving, and providing opportunities for high performers to advance their careers. The selections that follow survey these and other skills and offer ideas for applying them.

For example, you'll find articles explaining how to uncover and support your best employees' career aspirations, as well as how to measure the value of retention for your company's bottom line. You'll also discover some startling facts; for example, pay *isn't* the most powerful motivator for most employees. Finally, you'll learn about five fundamental competencies that will help you build your reputation as a "manager of choice" for loyal, engaged workers.

Why Retention Should Become a Core Strategy Now

• • •

Paul Michelman

It's 12:05 p.m. on a Wednesday, and Jeff Taylor, founder of the online job marketplace Monster, is running late. His assistant sticks her head in the door of his office and urges him to move on to his next appointment: the employee lunch, an open-discussion meal that Taylor hosts every other month. On Tuesday, Taylor spent the morning in an orientation session for 27 new hires. Later in the week, he'll be serving as DJ at a companywide outing, a payback to employees after last year's holiday party was cancelled because it seemed like too much of an extravagance. Staff at the company have something else to celebrate these days: merit raises were recently awarded.

For Jeff Taylor and like-minded leaders, a focus on morale and retention isn't just about maintaining a positive work atmosphere during these tough times. Nor is it simply about making sure that your best people remain committed to the firm should the market soon beckon with new opportunities. It's about establishing a way of doing things that may well be essential to survival just a few years down the road. According to a 2000 Bureau of Labor Statistics report, by 2010 there could be as many as 10 million more jobs available than there are employees in the United States—thanks to a combination of factors, including the retirement of baby boomers and a decrease in workers aged between 25 and 34.

You think 1999 was a bad time to be hiring? That year "was only a footprint for what we'll see in 2008," Taylor says. "We'll be facing the worst labor shortage in our lifetime within the next five years."

While many experts echo Taylor's thoughts about an impending labor shortage, there are others who believe that a combination of advancing technology and increasing globalism will mitigate its severity. Nevertheless, one day in the not-too-distant future the job market will swing back toward the job seeker's advantage. And when it does, the effect on some organizations—particularly those that let employee satisfaction and retention strategies take a back seat to seemingly more pressing issues of corporate survival—could be severe.

On a national stage, notes John A. Challenger, CEO of the outplacement firm Challenger, Gray & Christmas, "the mood is grim. For those who have managed to avoid job cuts, morale has definitely suffered. One recent survey [of U.S. workers] found that 34% of respondents were likely to leave their jobs once the economy improved." In addition, in an August 2003 study by Accenture, 48% of U.S. middle managers surveyed said they were looking for another job or planned to do so when the economy recovered.

So for those companies that believe the quality of their people is central to building value, it may be time to reconsider the "they have no place else to go" strategy of employee retention.

Many firms are doing just that, and they are finding that the key to retention is found in a strategy that considers both their employees' personal aspirations (career development, recognition, reward) and the aspirations they possess for their organizations.

Focusing on the Individual

Recovering from an approach that put retention low on the priority list won't necessarily be easy, says David Sholkoff, a principal in Deloitte & Touche's Human Capital Advisory Services practice. "By waiting until now to create employee initiatives, those initiatives may be seen as just initiatives. Or as one client told me, 'It seems that all of a sudden we are trying to focus on our employees. This is really just leadership being self-serving.' Those organizations that were not focused on their people are in a deficit position today."

However, he continues, "there is still hope. I think we are seeing more employees take an individual look at their jobs in the long term. They would rather remain with their current employer if career opportunities are presented. Thus, organizations that are serious about retaining key talent have a great opportunity today to create a work environment that allows for flexibility, growth, and development."

While a commitment to building this type of culture has to come from the top, experts say, much of the responsibility for retention rests with individual managers and their ability to employ Grade A people-management and motivation skills. Leaders who can enable meaningful and fulfilling work experiences for their teams are much more likely to win loyalty and retention—especially when times are tight and monetary rewards may be slim.

Senior executives and immediate supervisors alike need to ask some important questions of their top employees, says Sharon Jordan-Evans, coauthor with Beverly Kaye of *Love 'Em or Lose 'Em: Getting Good People to Stay.* "What can we do to keep you? What kinds of things do you want next in your career—e.g., the chance to learn something new, title change? Then, listen," she says. "Tell the truth about what you can and cannot give right now and ask, 'What else?' I guarantee there will be one thing he wants that you can give. If talented people really believe that you treasure them, count on them, and want to reward them (in many ways)—they're more likely to hang in there with you, even when the tide turns for the better."

Another powerful influencer of retention in which the manager's role is central is "providing work that best suits individuals' particular interests," says David Lewin, director of the Advanced Program in Human Resource

> "Being unavailable only sends the wrong message; no one wants to feel like they are being left in the dark or ignored."

Management at UCLA's Anderson School. "Individuals differ greatly in this regard. A company should exert some effort and undertake some analyses to determine the nonmonetary interests and preferences of its key employees, and then attempt to meet these preferences in action."

Striking a similar chord, Paul McDonald, executive director of Robert Half Management Resources, suggests that managers focus on getting their best people more deeply engaged and thus more committed to the organization. Managers should look to unleash the creativity of their top people by soliciting their ideas on how to improve the bottom line. At the same time, McDonald says, managers need to give their people a sense of empowerment by providing the breathing room to take risks, use their own best judgment, and be accountable for the decisions they make. He also stresses a greater need for open communication during tough times. "Being unavailable only sends the wrong message; no one wants to feel like they are being left in the dark or ignored. Be accessible to employees when they have questions, concerns, or ideas," he says.

Some organizations view managers' roles as so important to retention that they have established clear responsibilities and goals in this regard, including tying variable compensation to retention rates, but also rewarding managers who help good employees leave their groups for other jobs in the company, rather than holding them back and thus eventually losing them to outside firms.

Learning What People Want— For Themselves and the Firm

One company attacking the retention issue head-on is Quaero, which designs and implements CRM solutions and serves several Fortune 1000 companies. At Quaero an aggressive effort to reconnect with employees began with senior management recognizing that decisions stemming from the economic downturn could be putting the firm at risk with at least some of its workers.

As Quaero transitioned from growth to survival mode, the company's management had made some tough choices, including downsizing its consulting force, tightening decision making and communication, emphasizing company needs ahead of individual development goals in making assignment decisions, making temporary salary cuts, and replacing expected cash bonuses with stock options in 2001.

Looking at their situation in the most negative light possible, says HR director David Drysdale, "some employees might conclude that they have been taken for granted in that they have demonstrated incredible commitment" to an organization that has not recognized them appropriately. They haven't received financial gains, their professional aspirations haven't been responded to, and the company "has become less inclined to really involve them in the business in a meaningful way," he says.

Acknowledging this, Quaero's commitment to improve morale and boost engagement involves several simultaneous efforts. Among them: one-on-one meetings; a commitment to top-down improvement in communication and information sharing; a shift toward more flexible working schedules; and actual payment of quarterly cash bonuses, subject to meeting published net income targets.

Just as importantly, the firm is deploying a company-wide employee commitment survey in an effort to establish a clear baseline of employee opinion and priorities. The survey asks employees to respond to a lengthy series of questions, both general and quite granular, that Drysdale hopes will paint a meaningful picture of how Quaero's people view the organization and their roles in it. The majority of the questions ask employees to rate their degree of agreement with statements such as these:

- I expect to remain working at Quaero for at least the next two years, assuming I continue to meet performance expectations.

- I would recommend Quaero to my friends as a good place to work.

- Quaero's values are consistent with my personal values.

- There are no process or organizational barriers to my doing a good job.

- The work that I do makes a difference to this organization.

- Our leadership team has the capabilities and commitment to address the challenges Quaero faces.

- I am trusted to make meaningful decisions in my day-to-day activities.

- I am paid fairly given my responsibilities and performance.

The survey concludes with open-ended questions such as "What one thing could we start to do as an organization that would have the biggest impact for our clients and our people?" that allow for a greater expression of employee opinion.

Other firms are conducting employee culture surveys as well as companywide "stay interviews," in which managers let people know how important they are to the company and ask what kinds of things will keep them.

At Quaero, the linchpin is that management made a public commitment to act on the results of the survey before its launch. "It isn't really the conducting of surveys that promotes retention, it's what companies do in response to what they learn that counts," Drysdale says. "The way in which the survey will promote retention is that addressing the issues it may raise will help move all of our people to the point at which they are so engaged in what they are doing that they will have neither the time nor the inclination to look around or, as important in an up market, to take calls from recruiters."

It's too soon to judge the impact of Quaero's employee survey. However, the company has already seen some initial success in its efforts to re-engage staff, Drysdale notes. For example, the firm completed a quick-hit survey specifically about benefits, which led to a change in the firm's benefits brokers, as well as its medical, vision, and dental insurers, improving features and service levels while aggressively capping rate increases.

"How at risk do we feel of losing key people as the job market upswing comes?" he asks. "This is a tough one. We recognize the risks and are taking actions to address them. Morale overall is probably to some degree the same as the economy overall—at a tipping point. It is on an upswing, but a shallow one, and our challenge is to steepen the slope of that curve."

Building a Culture of Retention

"In good markets and bad, there are always opportunities for top performers," says Frank Brown, global leader for Assurance and Business Advisory Services for Pricewaterhouse Coopers (PwC). "The real trick is creating a culture that sustains all employees," says Brown, one that will "engender a positive response to questions like these: Is my work valued? Does my opinion count? Are new ideas welcomed? Are people treated with respect? Am I evaluated and rewarded on my performance? Does leadership act with integrity?"

The desire to create that kind of environment has

prompted PwC to create a number of programs focusing on its people.

For instance, PwC's Australian business introduced an initiative 16 months ago called High Performance Culture that aims to inspire and develop staff by driving the organization's values into everyday business behaviors, Brown says. Leaders hand-deliver staff employment offers personally, and at offices throughout the country,

> **"In good markets and bad, there are always opportunities for top performers."**

top management walk the halls ringing bells to publicly acknowledge high achievers.

But culture change won't work if it's solely directed from above, Brown notes. "It also needs to bubble up naturally from below as people embrace new behaviors and attitudes." Brown describes the new type of culture that PwC strives for as one less dependent on rules, hierarchy, and tradition, and more attuned to performance, innovation, and change.

To that end, and to build retention among its top performers, PwC has invested heavily in a leadership development initiative called Genesis Park. The program identifies six to nine top performers from a variety of client-facing practices around the world, Brown says; takes them off billable revenue-generating client work (this removal constitutes a major investment for the firm); and puts them together as a team for five months. The program includes business case development, strategic projects and thought leadership, team building, change management, and in-depth discussions with business leaders from PwC and other companies.

More than 60 people from 19 countries have participated in the program to date. According to Brown, "Graduates report feeling more connected to the firm and its leaders, a greater sense of commitment to their jobs, a better understanding of relevant business issues, and a deeper sense that they are recognized for their ideas and contributions and have a real stake in the firm's success. Just as important, graduates carry this enthusiasm back to the people they work with."

In the two and a half years of the program's existence, the cumulative retention rate among Genesis Park alumni stands at 98% compared with an annual retention rate of 75% for their peers, Brown says.

Bottom-line Benefits, Whatever the Market

For all the myriad approaches companies take to promote loyalty among their employees—broad-based and narrow, short-term and long-term—the one universal truth is that employees are more likely to stick it out in tough times when they feel that they are treated with integrity.

"There is no reason that companies cannot retain and/or rebuild favor among employees," Challenger says. "We see countless examples of companies that are able to go through significant downsizings and those remaining, as well as those who were let go, still have positive feelings about the employer. It comes down to how people are treated. If they believe that the company is being fair and honest, they will endure downsizings, salary freezes, cuts in benefits, and no bonuses."

Reprint U0310A

Aligning Human Capital with Business Strategy

Perspectives from Thought Leaders

• • •

Cassandra A. Frangos

Human capital is now firmly acknowledged as a strategic source of value creation—indeed, a company's most valued asset—in today's knowledge-based economy. As natural custodians of human capital, human resource executives are expected to lead its development, but most HR organizations lack a strategic planning process for human capital, much less a consistent way to describe and measure it. A recent BSCol conference featured three leading voices on these issues: Dr. Jac Fitz-enz, the father of human capital benchmarking; David Norton, co-creator of the Balanced Scorecard (and author of a groundbreaking framework for human capital measurement and management); and Helen Drinan, then-CEO of the Society of Human Resource Management.

Measuring, Tracking, and Benchmarking the ROI of Human Capital

Dr. Jac Fitz-enz

Reflecting a growing view among leading thinkers, Jac Fitz-enz believes the HR organization will never achieve full potential until it can describe the role human capital plays in creating organizational value and demonstrate its investment return. Armed with such data, HR practitioners can identify and analyze relationships between business actions and human capital results. This is hardly bean-counter thinking; employee costs can exceed 40% of corporate expense. Add to that the investment in talent, development of organizational knowledge, and the fact that training time hasn't diminished nearly as rapidly as product and business cycles have accelerated, and you can see that turnover costs have mushroomed.

Traditionally, HR has reported on its ability to reduce the costs of HR processes, rather than focusing on the results. HR, like every business function, should have a set of operational metrics. Yet most functional areas lack metrics that describe their effectiveness in creating value. Just as an accounting system tells us what is happening by reporting profits and losses, there is a basic methodology for process management. Fitz-enz cited five generic ways to evaluate an HR process: How much does it cost? How long does it take? How much was accomplished? How many errors or defects occurred in the process? And, how did employees respond (e.g., to the job satisfaction survey)? Each of these criteria can be applied across the three core human capital practices: acquiring talent (cost per hire), developing it (cost per trainee), and retaining it (cost of turnover). Fitz-enz also advocates that organizations involve HR more actively in strategic planning. And if HR's mission is to improve business operations—to become a strategic partner—HR professionals must, as he says, "get their heads out of the paper and their minds in the business." The Balanced Scorecard can establish a common language and focus for demonstrating human capital's impact on desired business outcomes. Managing human capital effectively will help organizations execute their strategic plans. Start with the enterprise, he says, cascade to the business units and functions, and then show the value created from human capital. Measurement is the fuel for the

Balanced Scorecard, and human capital is the driver of strategy—and ultimately, success.

Measuring and Managing Human Capital: Getting to the Strategy Table

David P. Norton

HR executives have long been concerned with the question, "How do I get to the strategy table?" A recent study by Kennedy Information,[1] the leading research firm on the consulting industry, found that 40% of HR executives are asked to sit at the strategy table, while 60% still play a passive or reactive role. Norton's conclusion: HR lacks the science and tools to describe and measure human capital (as many as 85% of organizations do not have an adequate way to describe human capital, according to a BSCol survey of HR executives). Without the ability to measure HR's strategic contribution, organizations cannot manage human capital as a strategic asset. It's little wonder that half the organizations BSCol surveyed stated that human capital is not linked to strategy.

The Balanced Scorecard, though, has emerged as an important tool to address this challenge. The missing link between HR and the enterprise, Norton observes, is a shared model of the strategy. Such a model would give HR professionals a point of reference for defining the impact of human capital on organizational strategy—

and for tailoring development programs to the organization's strategic priorities. The Balanced Scorecard is the "how" that transforms the HR function from sideline player to strategic partner.

Three of the four BSC perspectives are based on time-tested management models: the financial perspective is based on the DuPont ROI model, the customer perspective on value propositions, and the internal perspective on value chains. But the learning and growth perspective, which encompasses intangible assets like human

Highlights from the Society of Human Resource Management Study
The Future of the HR Profession

Outstanding HR leaders...

- Derive their agenda from the company's business objectives.
- Focus on a few strategic priorities.
- Create a shared understanding with the CEO on HR's strategic, value-creating (rather than just tactical) ability.
- Stay in touch with the workforce; understand drivers of employee commitment and performance.
- Move HR away from "customer service" ("What do I have to do to meet expectations today?") and toward "customer focus" ("How can I take the

capital, lacks a standard management framework. Every HR professional has a different view of the important components of human capital (e.g., leadership, skills). A common framework would facilitate the development of standardized measures and benchmarks—and a common language—that would foster knowledge-sharing among HR professionals.

In 2001, BSCol formed the HR Action Working Group, a group of HR executives from more than 20 leading organizations. They worked together to define just such

---

HR function in a new direction over a period of time?").
- Build their business knowledge and financial and consulting skills.

What will HR look like in the next decade?

- Utilization of technology will be essential, not only to free HR from administrative work, but to help leverage information about the workforce.
- Thus enabled by technology, HR will play a more managerial role.
- HR departments will likely be smaller, more focused, and have greater impact on the business.
- If HR does not fulfill its strategic role, it will default to its historical role—transactional—and non-HR professionals will take the lead.

© 2001 The Society of Human Resource Management (text edited for space considerations)

a framework. The group identified five dimensions of human capital that executives find most relevant to their strategies:

- Strategic Skills/Competencies

- Leadership

- Culture and Strategic Awareness

- Strategic Alignment

- Strategic Integration and Learning

The starting point, they found, is to build a strategy map to articulate organizational strategy and then define how human capital is linked to strategy. This strategy-based view of human capital provides a prescriptive framework to guide the development of measures of the contribution of human capital. Out of this framework arose the "Human Capital Readiness Report," which provides a snapshot of an organization's human capital relative to its strategic requirements. It documents the strategic requirements, then shows, through its measures and programs, how human capital is being developed. HR professionals can use the report as a communications tool that, among other things, can help justify the value of human capital investments, something they are under increasing pressure to do. The report provides the foundation for a periodic review of HR's strategic challenges and contributions—in effect, a progress report. As such, it becomes the bridge between enterprise strategy and HR, giving HR entrée to the strategy table and empowering it as a true strategic partner. HR can now work toward improving human capital readiness, and more broadly, toward enhancing the organization's ability to execute its strategy.

HR in the New Millennium: A Perspective from the Profession

Helen G. Drinan

The impact of technology, global competition, outsourcing, and a shrinking pool of qualified talent on the organization demand a new kind of HR leadership—strategic leadership. Is the HR profession up to the challenge? How aligned are HR professionals with the CEO's top priorities?

One million people in the United States identify themselves as HR professionals. Opportunities abound for forward-thinking HR professionals. But for those who ignore the skills, experience, and technology it takes to implement workforce strategies with bottom-line impact, survival is at stake. Both types fail to understand the macro business environment and long-term issues— a requisite step to building successful business-aligned HR strategy. This integrated worldview has never been more critical, given today's accelerated, globally competitive business environment, and increasingly service- and knowledge-based economy.

In a recent study, the Society of Human Resource Management (SHRM) addressed such key questions as: What is the most exciting work in HR today? What skills and experience levels are necessary for the successful HR professional? Within the next decade, what are the primary workplace challenges facing the HR profession? And will the HR profession as we know it survive? (See "Highlights from the Society of Human Resource Management Study, *The Future of the HR Profession.*")

Workforce issues are at the top of the CEO's agenda. The SHRM study also revealed the increasing recognition that people represent the only real competitive advantage a company can sustain—and that HR's "seat at the table" is already established. The question is: Will it be occupied by an HR professional—or someone else? Who will execute the human capital strategy?

Interest in HR issues has grown beyond the HR department; indeed, there's a growing acknowledgment that human capital management has become a requisite skill for CEOs. Consider a recent Conference Board study[2], which cited customer loyalty and competition for talent as two of the biggest CEO challenges. SHRM's study revealed that HR's pressing issues are: becoming a strategic partner, applying new technology, managing talent, recognizing and developing the employee's relationship to company brand, dealing with mergers and acquisitions and business reconfigurations, and reducing costs. Figure 1 illustrates the alignment of the CEO's

Figure 1. The Future of the HR Profession *Study*

The alignment between the CEO's concerns and HR's challenges is significant, offering HR great opportunities.

challenges and HR's "most compelling" work, showing great opportunities for HR. Nowhere, incidentally, do you see HR language; you only see business language.

So what is the profile of outstanding HR leaders? Among other things, they derive their agendas from enterprise business objectives; they stay in touch with the workforce; think "customer focus," not "customer service"; and concentrate on a few strategic priorities.

The Future of HR: Linked
to the Enterprise Strategy

A growing number of HR experts—Brian Becker, Mark Huselid, David Ulrich, Steve Kirn, John Boudreau, to cite a few—are searching for measures and systems, both quantitative and qualitative (behavioral), to better align HR strategy with business strategy. Jac Fitz-enz provides an "HR-out" view that looks at HR processes and describes the human capital value added. The Balanced Scorecard offers a framework to manage and measure human capital and provides an integrated strategic planning process for HR. David Norton provides a "strategy-in" view of measuring and managing human capital.

At the same time, more and more organizations are successfully integrating human capital management and HR strategy through the BSC. At Alterra Health Care, the percentage of employees who understand the company's strategy grew from 20% to 80%. Hilton Hotels increased customer satisfaction as well as post-stay loyalty. It also shares company stock with employees. Crown Castle International transformed the HR function into a human capital partner, and Ingersoll Rand overhauled its strategic management system and aligned the organization using the Balanced Scorecard, with HR as leader and champion of the process.

It is clear that human capital is a strategic priority; what's not is how it will be managed. But if these positive developments are any indication, we should expect to see more of the strategy table seats occupied by HR in the not-too-distant future.

Notes

1. The Human Capital Market: Implications for HR Consultants (*Kennedy Information, December 2001*)

2. The CEO Challenge: Top Marketplace and Management Issues (*The Conference Board, January 2001*)

For Further Reading

The ROI of Human Capital: Measuring the Economic Value of Employee Performance by Jac Fitz-enz (2000, AMACOM)

"Measuring the Contribution of Human Capital," (*Balanced Scorecard Review*, Jul–Aug 2001), and "Managing the Development of Human Capital," (*Balanced Scorecard Review*, Sept–Oct 2001), both by David P. Norton

"Alterra Health Care's Fast Track to Results" by Janice Koch (*Balanced Scorecard Review*, Nov–Dec 2001)

Reprint B0205D

Employee Retention

What Managers Can Do

• • •

Today's brutal labor market has had at least one salutary effect: managers are waking up to the costs involved when a good employee walks out the door. Among them are:

DIRECT EXPENSES, including the out-of-pocket cost of recruiting, interviewing, and training a replacement. (And in this market, the replacement may require a higher salary than the one who's leaving—not to mention a signing bonus.)

INDIRECT COSTS, such as the effect on workload, morale, and customer satisfaction. Will other employees consider quitting? Will customers follow the employee who left?

OPPORTUNITY COSTS, including the knowledge that is lost and the work that doesn't get done while managers and other employees focus on filling the slot and bringing the replacement up to speed.

All told, experts estimate that replacing an employee is likely to cost twice the departee's annual salary. "Show these costs to senior management and they'll choke," says Sharon Jordan-Evans, coauthor of a new book on retention. "They'll say, 'What are we doing to keep these people—and who's responsible?'"

It's the Manager

Line managers in the past could mostly assume they weren't responsible. Employees left because they didn't like the company or because they had found a better job. They left to accompany a spouse to a new city. The manager's typical reaction—a shrug and a "what're you gonna do?"—wasn't a problem when departures were few and replacements plentiful.

Today, people leave jobs for all the old reasons and a host of new ones besides. They're going out on their own or they're joining a dot-com startup. A headhunter has called, and a competitor is offering a fat "golden hello." In recent months most labor markets have been so tight that employees can leave simply because they feel like trying something new—or because somebody looked at them crooked.

But whatever the proximate cause, something had to happen to make the employee even consider leaving.

And one big reason people do consider leaving, it turns out, is that a particular boss didn't do what he or she needed to do to keep them.

"Our research consistently validated the reality that *the manager plays a significant role in influencing the employee's commitment level and retention,*" state Dr. B. Lynn Ware and Bruce Fern, retention specialists with Integral Training Systems (ITS). Similarly, the Gallup Organization's

Watch Out! The Early Warning Signs of Defection

Are some of your people considering leaving? B. Lynn Ware, founder of retention consulting firm ITS Inc., counsels clients to watch for early signs of dissatisfaction and disaffection, including:

A change in behavior, such as coming in later or leaving earlier.

A decline in performance.

Sudden complaints from a person who hasn't been a complainer.

Wistful references to other companies. ("Something like, 'I heard of this guy who got a $30,000 signing bonus at a dot-com.'") Wistful references to other employees who left. "One of the things we look at is the whole domino effect, like when a manager or a multiyear study of 80,000 managers in 400 companies found that an employee's relationship with her direct boss is more important for retention than companywide policies such as pay and perks. "An employee may *join* Disney or GE or Time Warner because she is lured by their generous benefits package and their reputation for valuing employees," write Marcus Buckingham and Curt Coffman in their book analyzing the study. "But it is her

significant peer in an organization leaves. That can be a definite trigger."

Withdrawing from others. "Someone has been participating in meetings, maybe volunteering for extra projects, and now they're doing just enough to get by."

Talk about "burnout."

What if you see an early warning signal? "Arrange to meet privately with the employee right away," advises Ware. "Explain what you've noticed and ask if there's a deeper concern behind the complaints or behavior." Then tell the employee how much you value him, and ask for help in changing things. "You might say something like, 'I really want to see you have a better work experience than you have had recently. How do you think we can solve these problems?'"

The key: addressing the issue rather than ducking it. "Don't be nervous about bringing it up," says Ware.

relationship with her immediate manager that will determine *how long she stays. . . .*"

Managing for Retention: A Checklist

So what can managers do to keep as many good employees as possible? The steps are numerous, but they fall into three broad categories.

Create a Great Environment

Managers often assume that company policies and corporate culture determine the working environment. So they do, to an extent. But policies can be circumvented or changed—and ultimately the atmosphere in a department or unit is more important to individual employees than the culture of the corporation as a whole. How does your unit stack up on measures such as the following?

No Jerks Allowed. "It's easy to be a jerk," says Beverly Kaye, coauthor with Sharon Jordan-Evans of the new book *Love 'Em or Lose 'Em.* "A jerk is someone who never says 'thank you.' Someone who never says, 'How's your kid doing? I heard he was sick.' Someone who slams the door or gets in a bad mood."

Jerks can be recognized precisely because people don't stick around. "I don't like to bad-mouth my boss," a young MBA named Sharon told the Gallup researchers,

"... but I do know this: When I came here there were thirteen of us on his team. Now, a year later, every single one of them has left, except me." Concludes Jordan-Evans: "People with choices will not work for a jerk."

Friendly Relations. The opposite of jerkdom? Ordinary human virtues such as courtesy and respect—plus the recognition that workplaces are social settings, and

What About Poor Performers?

It's hard for most managers to let anyone go. It's doubly hard in a tight labor market, when you know it might take months to find a replacement. But retention experts don't advocate keeping someone on just to warm a chair. Having too many poor performers "creates demoralizing down-cycles," says Gerry Ledford, a practice leader in employee performance and rewards with Sibson & Co. "They clog up opportunities. And they don't perform well, which has an effect on overall corporate performance."

Better, says Ledford, to identify weak performers, develop an action plan that gives them a chance to improve—and then quickly take action if things aren't working out. "Give them help in outplacement. Give them unreasonably generous severance packages." The company will be the better for it. If the departing employee can find a job that suits him better—and these days he has a good chance—so will he.

that managers who take an interest in employees can engender an appealing atmosphere. "What kept me at that company for many years was really a simple thing," a furniture-retailing employee told Kaye and Jordan-Evans. "Every Friday we'd get together at a local pub and the general manager would come in and start the party with one question, 'So, how was your week?' . . . Mostly we just vented. [But] the amazing thing was, he was truly interested. We went home those weekends feeling great."

How Committed Are Your Employees?

Think all your employees are toiling happily in the vineyards of your company? If they're anything like the national average, forget it. According to a 1999 study of 2,000 employees by Hudson Institute and Walker Information:

33%, or about one in three, are "high risk"—that is, not committed to their present employer and not planning to stick around for the next two years;

39%, or about four in ten, are "trapped": they aren't committed to the organization, but they are currently planning to stay for the next two years; and

only 24%, or about one in four, are "truly loyal," both committed to the organization and planning to stay on for at least two years.

Source: Hudson Institute/Walker Information, "Commitment in the Workplace: The 1999 Employee Relationship Report Benchmark Study"

Peter Cappelli, a professor at the University of Pennsylvania's Wharton School who has studied retention, advocates building more elaborate social communities. "Loyalty to companies may be disappearing," he writes in *Harvard Business Review*, "but loyalty to colleagues is not." Thus companies such as Ingage Solutions have reduced turnover among notoriously mobile software engineers by creating golf leagues, investment clubs, and softball teams. Now, points out Cappelli, "leaving the company means leaving your social network of company-sponsored activities."

Information Sharing. Freely dispensed information—about the business, about financial performance, about strategies and plans—tells employees that you trust them with the data, and that you respect their ability to understand and contribute to the business as a whole. Your organization may not be completely open-book, say Kaye and Jordan-Evans, but you yourself can share what you know about its strategic direction and internal workings. What's more, if you hear of something that people are likely to find out—the resignation of a prominent manager, say—tell your employees now, not later.

Create Great Jobs

United Parcel Service, Cappelli observes, restructured its delivery jobs so that drivers—whose knowledge and know-how are critical to the company's success—aren't responsible for the tedious task of loading trucks. At Prudential, an experimental program encourages managers to tailor jobs to individuals' interests. But you don't need such companywide initiatives to begin reshaping your employees' job descriptions. Some watchwords:

Allow Autonomy. Many people enjoy working with a minimum of supervision. Send a team off on its own with the charge of exploring a new market or solving a business problem. Carve out a whole business unit and let its members work on their own. "We're the number one company in the annuity business," says Ann de Raismes, senior VP of human resources for Hartford Life. "And that business was built by a group of people that were given tremendous amounts of freedom and autonomy. It's important you create that type of environment."

Let People Stretch. Most people also enjoy a challenge—and the feeling that their boss is entrusting them with bigger responsibilities than they had a right to expect. "Put people in jobs before they're ready," advises McKinsey & Co.'s 1998 report "The War for Talent." Hartford Life's de Raismes concurs. "We give people stretch assignments, sometimes before they're ready. But if you really believe in people and you properly support them and they've got the right attributes, I believe that nine times out of ten people are going to be successful. Sixty percent of our executives have a new assignment

Let Them Leave—But Keep Them in the Company

"Within our organization we have a lot of really bright people who are very talented and recruitable," says Lisa Dunlap, VP for retention and recruiting of Thomson Corp., a 40,000-employee company. Dunlap wanted to make sure they knew of every available opportunity within the company, so that those who wanted to change jobs would stay with Thomson.

The tool: Thomson Career Center, an online job-posting service that advertises 800–1,000 openings a month. Employees can create "personal search agents" on the site that notify them electronically of jobs they might be interested in. A series of "career road maps" offers tips for managing employees' careers. Dunlap let employees know of the new center through "electronic postcards, posters in the offices, a CD-ROM launch kit, user guides for employees, and user guides for HR professionals." The usage so far: 5,400 unique visits per month.

every 12 to 18 months. You have to do that in order to keep talent."

Be Flexible. A survey last year by Ceridian Employer Services confirmed what savvy managers have learned by experience: flexible work arrangements are "highly successful" in retaining employees. Nearly two-thirds of

First Step to Retention: Hooking the Hottest Prospects

One key to retention is crafting a job offer that attracts the people you want and who will fit best with your company. The most successful offers are "holistic"— that is, they include at least four distinct points of appeal:

Money. Make your offer in terms of total pay, advise Jay Schuster and Patricia Zingheim, principals of a compensation consulting firm that bears their names. Total pay includes base salary, bonus, all forms of equity, and benefits. Add them all together and you can impress the candidate with just how much you're willing to spend to land her.

Personal growth. Career growth and personal development are important to nearly all job candidates. So be sure they get a chance to hear about advancement opportunities, along with training and development programs offered by your company. "Let prospects see who gets ahead in your company, who succeeds in this place," says David Dotlich of CDR International, Inc., a consulting firm specializing in cultural issues. America Online assigns a "buddy for a day" when hot prospects come to visit. Biotech leader Amgen partners candidates with different employees at each meal during their on-site visits.

Worklife. Communicate the quality of your company's worklife and environment—internal traits such as its culture and atmosphere, external factors such as the community, recreational opportunities, and school system. The traditional site visit is still the most effective way to pitch worklife—and now companies are offering prospects two or more trips, sometimes including the candidate's entire family. Fast-growing telcom company Tellabs invites key candidates and their families to spend a weekend in nearby Chicago so they can get a feel for the Windy City. Amgen does the same in Los Angeles. Amgen also gives candidates access to a network of newly hired employees. "Singles can talk to other singles, spouses to other spouses," explains Thomas Hutton, Amgen's associate director of staffing. "They can get an inside look at the recent experiences of other people who have accepted our offers."

Corporate future. Everyone wants to work for a winner. Your company's reputation, its values and vision, its past record, and its plans for the future are all part of this recruiting hook. Tailor the pitch to the candidate as necessary. For job candidates from within the biotech industry, Amgen's recruiters pitch the security and resources of the company's leadership position. For those from the more mature pharmaceuticals industry, they pitch the entrepreneurial aspects of an aggressive young company.

(continued)

Finally, find the individual candidate's favorite bait. "The days of the generic interview process and compensation package are over," says Ranell Durgan, AOL's senior director of strategic staffing. "We are selling the company and assessing the candidate's needs at the same time, approaching each individual as a unique case." AOL's recruiters begin working to understand the candidate before the first direct contact. They think of the process as preparing for a cold sales call by learning everything possible about a prospect. Then, "whether it's equity, career path, or flexibility, go in with some kind of hook," advises Durgan. "Explain the opportunity, hit the hot points, and hook them."

Ceridian's respondents felt that virtual teams, flexible work plans, and telecommuting were effective in boosting retention. To be sure, not every manager has the authority to create whole new work arrangements. But nearly everybody can allow some on-the-spot flexibility—letting employees rearrange work to care for a sick child, for example, or to keep a doctor's appointment. Today's harried employees value that kind of flexibility highly.

Ask Early; Ask Often

Great work environments and great jobs are a matter of opinion; what challenges one person may terrify another. So you won't know how well you're doing on either score unless you ask.

Don't Wait for the Exit Interview. Companies routinely ask departing employees why they're leaving. But exit interviews "just scratch the surface of the causes [of] attrition," argue ITS's Ware and Fern. For example, employees are likely to report what's attractive about the new job (more money, say) without explaining why they were looking in the first place (which may have had nothing to do with compensation).

Instead of waiting, hold the conversation now. "Sit your employees down one at a time, face to face, and say to them, 'You are so important to me, I want to know how to keep you,'" advises Sharon Jordan-Evans. "Always make it a plural: 'What are the kinds of things that will keep you? What kinds of opportunities, growth, etc. do you want?' Sometimes by phrasing it that way, you avoid the one answer 'I want a raise,' which is what managers are afraid of. What we know—and what our research supports—is that it isn't about more money. People get more money and they still go because all those other things that matter more than money are missing."

Get Feedback on the Work Environment. In addition to asking about individual goals, ask people how they like working in your unit. Do they feel included or excluded? Do they have suggestions for change? Hartford Life starts this process six months after an employee is hired, with a formal session asking what they think about the company. "Over the years we've made some changes based on that feedback," says Peggy

Holtman, director of employee development. "We enhanced our tuition reimbursement program. We made changes in the cafeteria. We made changes to our compensation plan." You can make changes in your unit based on what employees tell you.

And Get Feedback on Yourself. Employees leave "bad bosses"—but who among us is likely to admit that he or she is a lousy boss? That's the value of 360-degree assessment programs. "Arrow Electronics uses its 360-degree feedback system, monitored by CEO Steve Kaufman himself, to determine whether managers are actually providing the feedback and coaching that they should," reports McKinsey.

If you don't have a 360-degree program—and if your employees aren't already leaving in droves—you may not be aware of your weak points. Of course, it's tough to get honest assessments of your performance as a manager; people don't like to offer face-to-face criticisms, especially of their bosses. One good technique: explain to your direct reports that you really want their honest assessments of your performance, and that you've asked a trusted third party (perhaps someone from HR) to interview them. Assure them that you'll hear—and pay attention to—the criticisms, but that you won't know where they originated.

Despite all your best efforts, some people will leave. "You can't counter the pull of the market," advises Cappelli; "you can't shield your people from attractive opportunities and aggressive recruiters." But you can have an influence on how many people leave and when. The better job you do at building a great unit, the less likely you are to lose the very people you want to keep.

For Further Reading

Love 'Em or Lose 'Em: Getting Good People to Stay by Beverly Kaye and Sharon Jordan-Evans (1999, Berrett-Koehler Publishers)

First, Break All the Rules: What the World's Greatest Managers Do Differently by Marcus Buckingham and Curt Coffman (1999, Simon & Schuster)

"A Market-Driven Approach to Retaining Talent," by Peter Cappelli (*Harvard Business Review,* January–February 2000)

Reprint U0004A

How to Keep Your Company's Star Employees

• • •

Edward Prewitt

Managers have recently been pouring huge amounts of energy into strategies for retaining employees. But the strategies aren't working. According to a new survey by consulting firm Kepner-Tregoe, turnover problems are getting worse, not better. Nearly two-thirds of the 1,290 managers and employees participating in the survey reported that turnover in their organizations has actually increased over the last three years, despite a variety of attempted countermeasures.

Of course, there are some people any manager would

be happy to lose. But what happens when your star performers—the 20% of employees who do 80% of the work—start leaving? "Retaining talent has become the top-line issue these days," says Brian Hackett, senior program manager of HR research at the Conference Board in New York City. The majority of Kepner-Tregoe respon-

> At Cypress Semiconductor, CEO Rodgers has set up a formal procedure for responding to a star employee's defection.

dents reported that the loss of high-performing employees had dulled their companies' competitive edge and led to a decline in quality and customer service.

To be sure, companies aren't letting fast-track employees go gently into that good job market. Signing and stay-on bonuses, stock options, generous and flexible benefits, expansive training programs, even liberal moving allowances and job-search assistance for spouses are now common policies to boost retention, according to Jim Harris and Joan Brannick, authors of the new book *Finding and Keeping Great Employees*. But what works and what doesn't? A trio of recent studies—along with some insights from companies that somehow keep their best people despite the tightest labor market in years—suggests some answers.

Pay: The "Least Important" Factor

Hay Group, the big HR consulting firm, recently released the results of a survey of half a million employees from more than 300 companies. The study compared the satisfaction of "committed" employees—those who said they would stay with their organization for more than five years—with the attitudes of employees who planned to leave within a year. Of the 50-plus factors analyzed, "pay was the *least* important," says David A. Hofrichter, VP and managing director in Hay's Chicago office. "Which is an important finding, because a lot of people look there first. They say, 'We need signing bonuses, we need big raises, we need equity.' There's a place for all that...but when the environment's good, people will work for less pay."

The other studies support these conclusions. Two-thirds of the managers and workers surveyed by Kepner-Tregoe said their organizations had boosted salaries and other financial rewards to try to stem turnover. But most didn't think money was among the top reasons for the departure of high-performing employees. Harris and Brannick, who studied dozens of companies with low turnover, conclude bluntly that "for the vast majority of employees money is not the primary motivator."

SAS Institute, a software company, has a legendarily low turnover rate—less than 5% a year over the company's 23-year history—in an industry that averages a 20% turnover rate. The company pays competitive salaries but eschews whopper bonuses and stock options. (SAS is privately held.) "I'm not convinced that compensation ideas, direct or indirect, are at the core of why people work and what makes them stay," says VP of human resources David Russo. "Our perspective is that, although money is important, what people really want is recognition and a place they're proud to work. . . . If the work environment is somewhat toxic, [pay] holds people's feet to the fire for only so long."

Then, too, an emphasis on pay can be corrosive to a company. T. J. Rodgers, CEO of Cypress Semiconductor, routinely raises the salary packages of his star employees to repel competitors' offers, but declares that "If you use salary as the only measure, you're virtually guaranteed to have a collection of prostitutes, and just as quickly as they jumped fence for you, they'll go somewhere else as soon as someone offers them more money."

One Key: Learning Opportunities

Of all the factors in employee retention identified by Hay, the single most important was the opportunity to learn new skills. Dissatisfied employees—those planning to jump ship within a year—tended to say, "I'm in a job that doesn't allow me to learn and use new skills. I'm not growing here," according to Hofrichter. Again, best-practice companies already know this. "We try to encourage people not to chase pay but [instead] to chase responsibilities and learning opportunities," says Mike Croxson, senior VP for HR at Synovus Financial Corp., whose turnover rate of 12% is about half the industry average. "There are very few voluntary departures of senior managers."

Another View: Should You Focus on Stars at All?

Behind the concern with "stars" is the assumption that some employees are important enough to be singled out. That's a difficult assumption for many managers, notes David A. Hofrichter of the Hay Group, adding that organizations "need to be comfortable with the idea that they're going to treat top performers differently, because those kinds of people contribute most to the company." According to Kepner-Tregoe's study, "Retention Leader" companies have overcome any such discomfort. "Retention Leaders do not need to be reminded that their 'stars' set the tone and carry the load for the rest of the workforce," says the Kepner-Tregoe report.

But some executives of low-turnover companies argue that a star system can be counterproductive. The reason: singling out top performers can actually hasten their departure while alienating other people. "If you tell me I'm a high performer—one in ten—I'm going to tell that to a headhunter," say Mike Croxson of Synovus Financial. At SAS Institute, says Dave Russo, "We have

Feedback—Especially for Stars

Another top factor uncovered by Hay was coaching and feedback from supervisors. "That's interesting, because [we find that] the people who get the least amount of feedback are the high performers," says Hofrichter.

avoided anointing people as stars and fast-trackers, although we have people with star talent."

At the heart of these objections is a focus on the team over individuals. Synovus and SAS (#1 and #3, respectively, on *Fortune*'s list of the 100 Best Companies to Work For) espouse similar corporate philosophies. "We're in the business of building leadership, not management," Russo explains. "It's not been our pattern to identify people as stars because we don't think that helps our organization." Synovus uses a balanced-scorecard approach to rate and guide the actions of its managers. "The scorecard tells [managers], 'Your job is to make all the people under you successful,'" Croxson says. "We've worked hard to create systems that reflect the notion that success means, 'Forget yourself and focus on the team.'"

In this environment, singling out team members runs counter to fundamental precepts. As Croxson puts it, "You can't have a high-potential strategy and not believe that everyone's high-potential. I can't say, 'We're a high-potential company,' and then look at two people and say, 'You're high-potential and you're low-potential.' Folks on the team aren't stupid. They see the disconnect."

"[Their managers] think they don't need it—if they don't get that feedback, everything's going to go fine with their work." Ironically, high performers are the employees most interested in hearing feedback. "They're the ones planning their next move, thinking about the progress of their career. . . . And if they don't get it, they think, 'This company doesn't care.'" Harris and Brannick, who compiled eight best practices for retention from their research, say that one such practice is simply keeping employees in the loop. "The fastest way to transform a top-performing staff into a group of disgruntled, discouraged, job-seeking workers is to shut them out of the loop of corporate information."

Bad Bosses

"People don't leave companies, they usually leave bosses," says the Conference Board's Hackett. "That's where the deal breaks down. You might have a good tuition reimbursement program and do all these other programs right, but if a manager doesn't treat his or her direct reports right, then none of the other stuff matters." In the Kepner-Tregoe survey, 16% of respondents identified conflict with the boss as one of the three most common reasons for the departure of top-performing employees. What to do about bad bosses? Kepner-Tregoe lists "a stairstepping process for conflict resolution" among seven practices it found at companies effective in retaining employees: "A common practice among Retention Leaders is to offer legitimate alternate avenues that allow employees to circumvent their immediate supervisor, if necessary, and get their problems resolved." Motorola and Steelcase, for example, allow workers to take grievances all the way up to senior executives.

At Cypress Semiconductor, CEO Rodgers has set up a formal procedure for responding to a star employee's defection, culminating in a face-to-face meeting with Rodgers. "If you're a high-level manager in this company and you want to get in trouble with me," Rodgers says, "just let someone important leave without me having a crack at them." He adds that he's successful in changing employees' minds about half the time.

Rodgers goes to such lengths, he says, because "the value in a company increasingly is people. Money and resources have become readily available in our society—we're not limited by them anymore. It's all in people now."

For Further Reading

Avoiding the Brain Drain: What Companies Are Doing to Lock in Their Talent (1999, Kepner-Tregoe, Inc.)

The 1998–99 Hay Employee Attitudes Study (1998, The Hay Group)

Finding and Keeping Great Employees by Jim Harris and Joan Brannick (1999, AMACOM)

Reprint U9908B

Do People Want to Work for You?

• • •

Loren Gary

Companies know that their profitability improves when potential job seekers consider them an employer of choice. That's why they've devoted so much energy in recent years to developing not only the recruitment practices that will help them find the top talent they need to stay ahead of the competition, but also the retention practices that will keep current employees' hearts and minds engaged.

But organization-wide initiatives are not enough, according to consultant Nancy Ahlrichs, who's been studying employers of choice for the past seven years. "Many organizations I've studied had a gap even though they had a strategy for becoming an employer of choice in place." They just weren't able to attract and hang on to the most valuable workers. The reason for this gap, she says, is that a company's reputation as an employer of choice is only as strong as its individual managers.

Study after study supports this. An employee's relationship with his supervisor largely determines his view of the company. When the manager is seen as living out the company's vision and priorities, and taking an active interest in the employee's assimilation and growth, loyalty to the company soars. Alternatively, the top reason employees resign is because they don't get along with their boss.

In short, observes Ahlrichs in her book, *Manager of Choice: Five Competencies for Cultivating Top Talent,* a company cannot become an employer of choice (EOC) unless it has managers of choice (MOCs) throughout the organization who are faithfully implementing best practices in people management.

"We're not going to get great performance leaps from new business processes until we've achieved quantum leaps in managerial ability," says Ahlrichs. So what does it take to become an MOC, the manager sought by employees who have their choice of jobs and bosses? "Although a manager's education and technical skills play a role here," Ahlrichs continues, "what makes all the difference are people management skills that motivate employees to give discretionary effort—whether that's spending extra time with a customer or making additional phone calls. The potential for extra effort is always there, but it takes a relationship with a manager who understands more than project or budget management to put it into play."

MOCs who have this ability, Ahlrichs maintains, consistently excel in five fundamental competencies:

1. Talent scouting

2. Relationship building

3. Trust building

4. Skill building

5. Organization brand building

What follows is advice about how to improve on each of these fronts, along with insights from managers who've been recognized for their proficiency in these areas.

Talent Scouting

"When we see studies predicting that the available workforce in 2008 will be 15% smaller than it is today, we get concerned," says Bill Bagley, a director at Deloitte & Touche who oversees human resources for two regions. Such forecasts of a shrinking workforce make it all the more important for managers to have the right people in the right positions. Not only does your ability to bring in the best talent available help you upgrade your unit's competitiveness each time an opening occurs, but it also helps you keep the rest of your group engaged. The influx of new talent can help prevent the "knowledge ossification" that occurs when a team has been together too long.

> Make sure that your interviewing skills are as sharply honed as your other technical skills.

To get the best talent in the right places, you must see to it that candidates' "total job-shopping experience [with your group] stands out from that of other talent competitors," writes Ahlrichs. You can no longer afford to "passively outsource every aspect of the selection and hiring process to your HR department." Only by working closely with HR can you ensure that the finalists for a position possess more than just the necessary technical skills and experience. For Steve Kellam, CEO of B&D Navigator, the HR consulting arm of law firm Baker

& Daniels, this aspect of the search—identifying the candidates who have the attitude and the interpersonal skills that make for superior performance—is far more important than evaluating prior work experience.

Don't take an "I'll know the right candidate when I see him" attitude, cautions Ahlrichs. Instead, you've got to make sure that your interviewing skills are as sharply honed as your other technical skills. Give the greatest weight in your decision making to the competencies that characterize star performance in a particular position. Work with HR to identify the five to seven behaviors most critical to success in each position you're hiring for. If there are any incumbents in those positions who are star performers, talk to them individually to determine whether any additional behaviors they highlight should be added to your list.

Relationship Building

"Although many companies are doing a good job of talent scouting, I don't know that organizations as yet are paying enough attention in significant numbers to assimilating the talent they select," says Jack Robertson, a senior vice president and managing director of Right Management Consultants. "There's still a tendency to say, 'You were hired because you're supposed to be able to perform—why should we have to assimilate you?'"

Such an attitude reveals a common managerial blind

spot: although most managers have an appreciation for the role they play in helping employees develop their know-how—the hard skills required for technical competence—many are oblivious to the ways in which they can help employees develop the "know-who" they need to excel.

> When you've won employees' trust, they're more likely to stand by you during tough times.

An exercise that can help you get started in this work, Ahlrichs notes, is to give each of your reports a rating for each of the four types of workplace relationship they have: their relationship with you (the boss), their multiple relationships with their peers, their relationships with one or more other departments, and their various relationships with the community (customers, vendors, civic and professional organizations). Once you've got a bead on your reports' strengths and weaknesses, you can begin to devise strategies to help them improve.

Such strategies will, of course, need to be individually tailored. "Different people respond to different management and communication styles," says Kellam. "Instead of treating employees the way you want to be treated, treat them the way they want to be treated." And the only way to determine which approaches will work best with which employees is to maintain regular communication.

"Throughout my 46-year career in health care, my relationship development program grew out of meetings I'd hold with employees every six months," says Allan Hicks. "Even when I was head of a 1,000-bed hospital, I'd bring employees in in groups of 30 to 40 until everyone had had a chance to hear me discuss what we'd accomplished recently, what we were planning on doing over the next six months, and then to share their own ideas and concerns."

"Quite often there are things that need to be talked about that people are afraid to bring up," says Kellam. To help people get past this discomfort, he insists that each direct report bring to the regular face-to-face meeting a one-page memo describing what her current goals are, what she's accomplished since the past meeting, and what difficulties she may be having with Kellam, who prepares a similar memo for the meeting.

Trust Building

Surveys conducted by The Great Place to Work Institute indicate that managers looking to build a high-trust unit should focus on the following:

- CREDIBILITY. Make sure your communications are open and accessible. Demonstrate competence in your coordination of resources and integrity in carrying out the company's vision.

- RESPECT. Collaborate with employees on relevant decisions. Show appreciation for reports' efforts (never taking credit for their accomplishments), support for their professional development, and concern for their personal lives.

- FAIRNESS. Avoid favoritism in hiring and promotion. Make sure there's an appeals process for employees who believe they've been discriminated against.

- PRIDE. Show your admiration for your group's work and your respect for the company's products and standing in the community.

- CAMARADERIE. Be yourself—this makes it easier for your reports to do likewise. Foster a sense of team identity.

Managers who exhibit these characteristics see it as their responsibility to create opportunities for their reports to grow and develop. Robertson of Right Management Consultants remembers a former boss who groomed him from day one for three jobs beyond his current position: "Sometimes it would be simple stuff that he would do, such as including me in meetings that might have been above my level, as a way of increasing my comfort with the kinds of issues and challenges addressed there. The most fortunate experience you can have is to work for someone who trusts you and who gives you the freedom to grow. You wouldn't dare disappoint that kind of a boss."

When you've won employees' trust, they're more likely to stand by you during tough times. When Hicks saw that the competency of a hospital department he ran was subpar, he replaced the entire team. The trust he had built with the medical staff enabled him to do this. "Even though they didn't want to be a part of this action, the medical staff knew that the move had to be made."

Skill Building

"You either have 20 years of experience or one year of experience repeated 20 times," says Robertson. "Your hard skills will deteriorate without continual polishing."

To make it easier for employers not just to keep their skills up to date but also to add new ones, develop a mini-training function in your group, advises the consultant Ahlrichs. Create a learning task force charged with identifying the skills, behaviors, and knowledge group members need most to do their jobs better and meet unit goals. Through a variety of methods and media—lunch-and-learn sessions, discussion groups, a departmental library that compiles research from professional journals and Web sites, brief job shadowing and cross-training exercises—provide learning opportunities that are convenient, modular, and affordable. "Twenty to thirty minutes a day keeps overall learning moving forward," writes Ahlrichs.

But continuous learning is not sufficient, she adds: you must engage employees in continuous *teaching*, too. Teaching helps employees cement the knowledge they've just acquired, but perhaps even more important, it helps them improve the knowledge-transfer skills upon which organizations are increasingly reliant.

Organization Brand Building

Enhancing the organization's image in the mind of your reports should be at the top of your retention activities. Why? In a 2001 Towers Perrin survey, at least 56% of the nearly 6,000 respondents from mid- and large-sized companies in the U.S. and Canada said they were actively job searching or were open to another job. Moreover, a survey conducted by Right Management Consultants shows that until employees have been with a company for six years, their intention to stay remains below the level it was at during their first year in the organization. Not until the seventh year of employment does it rise above the first-year level. Translation: only by continually rerecruiting your current employees can you beat back other companies' efforts to hire them away.

Celebrate your employees as individuals. Remind them of the importance of their work to the company's strategic goals. And make sure they know about "your organization's efforts to make your community a better place for all," writes Ahlrichs—research into corporate philanthropy indicates that employees are five times as likely to stay when they have a favorable impression of their employer's philanthropic efforts.

Reprint U0403B

Engage Your Workers

• • •

Engaging your most talented people is a major element of retention and generates crucial benefits for your company. In the articles in this section, you'll discover powerful techniques for engaging valued workers. Performance reviews, for example, offer excellent opportunities to both praise good performance and invite employees to share their ideas and concerns about the work environment. Coaching—an interactive process by which you help your employees define and achieve their professional aspirations—is another potent engagement tool.

In this section, you'll also find guidelines for using

recognition and reward in creative ways to engage talented workers. Redefining definitions of what your people are expected to accomplish—in particular, challenging employees to take on increasingly complex tasks—can also boost motivation and performance.

Whose Job Is Employee Satisfaction?

• • •

Angelia Herrin

The management literature is full of advice for executives who want to deliver effective performance reviews of employees. The usual mantra? Use review sessions to set clear expectations and goals but never forget to praise good work and to listen closely to employee concerns.

So with all the good intentions, why do so many surveys find that employees are so miserable? A recent Towers and Perrin survey of 1,100 people from 1,004 companies, for instance, found fully a third felt "intensely negative" about their jobs and exhausted, confused, and unsupported in their offices.

The disconnect is real, says consultant Beverly Kaye. But it's not because managers deliver such bad reviews. Rather, employees aren't using review sessions to talk about what they want and need.

Reviews go awry, Kaye says, because too many employees lack the skills to focus their concerns, devise proposals for change, and make the business case for their requests—communication skills she believes companies should target in the review process.

These skills are particularly important now in a tight job market, she says, where some workers, feeling that they have nowhere to go, have simply "quit on the job": disengaging, producing less, and biding their time unhappily while making themselves and their coworkers miserable.

"Companies do employees surveys and then go to the HR people and to managers and say, 'OK, fix it,'" says Kaye, coauthor with Sharon Jordan-Evans of the book *Love It, Don't Leave It: 26 Ways to Get What You Want at Work*. "What we don't say to the employees is, 'We see what your complaints are—now you're going to have a major role in fixing them.'

"Workplace satisfaction is a two-way street. It's about the leaders and the managers, but it's about initiative and effort from employees, too."

Kaye, an employee retention expert who consults to Fortune 500 companies, recently surveyed 400 job switchers to learn why they left their organizations. She then went to their former bosses and told them the reasons their employees said they left. "Almost everyone said, 'Why didn't they tell me? I didn't know that; I could have done something,'" Kaye says. "It convinced me that smart companies need to approach the review process with two handbooks, not one."

What Do You Really Want?

If you want to get what you want as an employee, Kaye says, don't expect managers to take the first step, and never make them guess what you want—because they will most often guess wrong, even if they are well intentioned.

Kaye says that employees need to arrive at their review session with very clear ideas about what they want and how to ask for it—whether it's a job shift, a training program, a sabbatical, or a request for a change in a boss's behavior.

"The biggest mistake is not taking the time to plan," says Kaye. "Think of it as interviewing yourself: What do I want to accomplish? What's my agenda? What am I willing to say, and who will I have to convince?"

Managers need to coach employees to understand that declaring "I'm feeling dissatisfied" won't get much reaction, Kaye says, whereas offering a set of proposals to help solve a problem will get an immediate response.

"Remember, managers hear all day, 'Fix this, fix that,'" Kaye says. "You goal is to come in with a problem and some ideas about how to fix it."

A common misunderstanding managers have as review time approaches, she says, is that employees will ask only for money and promotion, when in fact what the employee is really looking for is validation and respect. Too often employees think money is the only thing to ask for, too.

> In making a request of your boss, lay out the WIIFT— what's in it for them.

In employee workshops, Kaye says she is told that it is easier to ask for money than appreciation. The problem, Kaye suggests, is that appreciation, dignity, and respect are so nebulous in contrast with money, which is so quantifiable. The best approach is to make a list of what appreciation would look like on the job, she says.

"Let's say you get reviews that say you are doing great, but most of the year, you feel ignored and overlooked," says Kaye. "Then be prepared to tell the boss you would like to have a note when you do something she likes." If that isn't her style, tell her you would like to have a cup of coffee every month and be told specifically what you have done well lately. In other words, let her know you want feedback in real time, not six months later.

"Stress the specifics," says Kaye. "Don't settle for 'You are good at your job.' Tell her that you want to hear specifically that it worked well when you did X or Y."

On the flip side, if a boss's behavior is demeaning or disrespectful, specifics will be even more important. "You can't just come in and say, 'You are too negative,'" says Kaye. "You need specifics, like 'When you criticize me in the hall in front of my team, it affects my ability to work effectively with them.'"

Making the Proposal

Employee surveys repeatedly find that employees feel "stuck" at work and believe that managers have not invested in their development. Kaye argues that employees need to get very specific with themselves and figure out if there is a development assignment or training program they need, and how it will prepare them for a desired job. This means doing research before the review to identify training opportunities and their costs, says Kaye. If the employee plans to request a job shift, she suggests working out a plan for making the transition and finding a replacement.

But while walking into the performance review with a well-researched, well-rehearsed plan for change is great, Kaye says, employees also need to remember to come equipped with several alternative plans for achieving their goals.

"The biggest mistake is coming with demands," says Kaye. "Instead, go in and say, 'Here's my problem, and here are three ideas I have for fixing it.' This way, you are giving the boss space.

"You show you've done your homework, but meanwhile you invite them to add more to the list. If you just walk in saying, 'I want to move up,' you push the boss in the corner." It is a lot harder to respond to a demand than to a selection of considered choices.

Closing the Deal

One of the simplest—and most overlooked—aspect of any employee request is laying out to the boss the WIIFT: what's in it for them, says Kaye.

Explain how your getting cross-training or taking a course, for instance, can help your boss and your unit be more effective. You also need to address the business case: What current business need will this change address? How will it increase value to the organization and contribute to the company mission? "It is also about explaining how your improved communication with superiors or your promotion to a more strategic job can help the company," says Kaye.

Be prepared to help the boss figure out what barriers may stand in the way of satisfying the request—whether they are people or budget problems or timing factors—and be ready to offer solutions.

"You probably have a pretty good idea of what might stand in the way—it's why you haven't asked for it before," says Kaye. "But if you've spent that much time thinking about the problems, you can probably figure out some other ideas for solving them, too."

Reprint C0401B

How
Great Managers
Manage People

• • •

Paul Michelman

The chain of events that leads to strong and sustained business results starts with great managers who defy common management practice at virtually every turn, says Curt Coffman, global practice leader for employee and customer engagement consulting at The Gallup Organization.

What is the defining contribution of great managers? They boost the engagement levels of the people who work for them. According to Gallup research, only 28% of U.S. employees are engaged, or are actively pursuing top performance on behalf of their organizations, and Gallup studies show that this has a direct impact on the bottom line. Engaged employees lead to engaged customers, who in turn drive a company's growth, long-term profitability, and stock price.

So what distinguishes managers who not only retain valuable employees but, by boosting engagement, also extract their full value? According to Coffman, coauthor with Marcus Buckingham of *First, Break All the Rules: What the World's Greatest Managers Do Differently*, the answer lies in rejecting conventional wisdom in four core areas of managing people: selection, expectation setting, motivation, and development.

Selection

Most managers select employees according to the skills needed for the role, but great managers select people for their talent. Coffman defines talent as a recurrent pattern of thought, feeling, or behavior and accounts for the different results produced by those with the same skills and training. Talent is abundant, Coffman observes, yet people whose natural talents fit their role are a rare and valuable commodity.

Consider what differentiates top-performing customer service representatives, Coffman notes. All reps in a firm get the same training, but the best take one-third fewer calls than the average to resolve the same complaint. Why? Because they use the phone as a tool of intimacy— they can envision what the customer looks like, what room he is in; they smile and nod even though the customer cannot see what they are doing. Instinctively, their talent leads them to manage each customer relationship in the most effective manner.

Great managers resist the temptation to hire people whose skills are a good match for how a job is already configured; instead, they seek those whose talent will redefine how the job is done.

Expectation Setting

Conventional wisdom says managers should specify the steps that employees need to take to accomplish a specific task. But great managers define the outcomes they seek and let each person use her individual talent to achieve them. For example, while great managers do not usually mandate steps to be taken, they do provide specific direction when accuracy or safety is involved, or when a company or industry standard is at stake. But even then they don't let the steps obscure the focus on the outcome.

Motivation

Conventional wisdom says that "anybody can be anything they want to be," and thus managers tend to focus on finding and fixing a person's weaknesses. This leads to reviews and development plans that focus on negatives—where the emphasis is on "improving" a person into someone he is not.

In contrast, great managers emphasize the development of their subordinates' unique strengths so as to help further their talent, while finding strategies to support their weaknesses. The key here is determining how to take greater advantage of what people already do well.

Development

Conventional managers rate the person and develop the performance; great managers rate the performance and develop the person—they realize that every person is different and should be treated as such.

Most companies view promotion as the natural path of progression. But is that always the right course? No, says Coffman, because success in one role is not necessarily an indication of success in another.

Consider how many outstanding account representatives fail miserably when they are promoted to sales managers. The ability to sell is entirely distinct from the ability to manage. What's more, promotion removes the high-performing salesperson from the position in which she has been producing substantial value for the company.

Great managers seek the right fit for a person's talent, they work to see that he is rewarded for his performance, and they endeavor to ensure that his talent is developed through progressively more challenging and meaningful assignments.

Reprint U0408B

How to Coach
Your Employees

* * *

Martha Craumer

Starting tomorrow, you'll be heading the financial services development team. You're charged with creating
a constant stream of clever new variations on well-
established products that have a long, successful track
record of sales with the public. You know the team
already, and most of them are the kind of people you
want—smart, creative, flexible, high-energy.

The guy who's been on the team the longest, Frank, is
a different story. He's everybody's favorite—probably because opposites attract. He doesn't seem to have a creative bone in his body. Frank's typical response to every
new idea the rest of the team throws at him is to ques-

tion whether or not the public really needs "another way to buy something that's been fine for 50 years." But he's conscientious to a fault, and the team relies on him to provide the research and the background reports that always seem to take more time than anyone else has to give them.

Just before you started your new role, the company instituted a new evaluation and bonus process that will reward your team on the number of new product ideas it can bring to market, and there's no question that Frank will drag the team down. If you can't find a way to use Frank productively, the rest of the team will resent him. How can you turn Frank into a creative powerhouse? He's already beginning to show signs of defensiveness—he knows the new evaluation scheme will eventually nail him.

This is not a problem you can manage Frank out of. Frank's weakness is his lack of creativity. And you can't just push uncreative people to be more creative. However, you might be able to coach him into greater productivity—or a different role on the team.

New insights gleaned from the rapid expansion of executive coaching over the past half-decade have practical implications for today's managers. Let's see what advice we can get from the experts that could be applied to Frank.

Managerial coaching is about getting the most out of your people by showing them that you respect and value them. "Good coaching avoids manipulation and coercion," explains Stan Hustad, performance coach and leader of the PTM Group. "Coaching asks what is *right* as well as what works."

Build Mutual Trust and Mutual Respect

According to James Flaherty, executive coach and author of *Coaching: Evoking Excellence in Others,* the successful coaching relationship has three interdependent elements: trust, respect, and freedom of expression. To get there, make sure your actions are consistent with your words. Don't tell others what your people have shared with you in confidence. Follow through on your promises and commitments. Be honest, objective, and fair. And remember, you don't have to "like" a person to build a mutually trusting and respectful relationship with them.

Ask Permission to Coach

Never mind that you're the boss. Show consideration and respect for your people by asking their permission to give them feedback. This can be as simple as saying, "May I offer a couple of suggestions?" or "Would you be open to taking a different approach to that problem?" By approaching your employees in this way, you're offering to share your power and control with them, in effect. And this, in turn, minimizes the likelihood of a defensive response.

Rethink Performance Goals

In the typical performance review, managers highlight areas of "weakness" that employees should try to improve. The goal is a "well-rounded" employee. In her new book, *Drive Your People Wild Without Driving Them Crazy*, Jennifer White explains, "You took their strengths, the skills they could have used to make a real impact, tossed them aside and had them focus their attention on getting better at their weaknesses. What you created was a dull group of people who look and act like everyone else. . . . No wonder you can't make real inroads on creativity or innovation with your team." A far better approach may be to overlook weaknesses and instead encourage and develop what your people do well naturally. White suggests that coaches look for areas in which their people can be superstars and present them with opportunities to really make a difference. A good coach looks for ways to leverage the strengths of his or her people. Should you really care that someone has a messy desk or is disorganized or introverted if that person is performing brilliantly in a critical area?

View "Weaknesses" as Strengths

Instead of seeing the shortcomings of your people as something to be corrected, try viewing them as the flip side of strengths. What you see as "wimpiness," for

97

Coaching Skills

To get the most out of your coaching sessions, brush up on these key skills:

Preparation. Don't wing it, even if your coaching session is informal. At the very least, go over in your head what the issues are, how you'll approach your team member, questions you'll ask, and follow-up actions to suggest. Every coaching interaction is an opportunity—don't leave the outcome to chance.

Observation and assessment. Observe how your people work and interact with others. What impact are they having on other members of the team or on overall goals and objectives? Avoid being judgmental or making assumptions and look for ways to test and confirm your observations.

Questioning. Open questions encourage participation and the sharing of ideas. Questions like "What would happen if . . ." help your people to explore options and see things from other perspectives. Closed questions—those that require a yes, no, or other short answer—confirm understanding and focus responses.

Listening. Good listening encourages open, honest communication. Put your work aside and focus on the person in front of you. Try to create a relaxed, accepting atmosphere and avoid interrupting or speeding the conversation along. Watch for nonverbal cues and body language that can help you read between the lines.

Feedback. As noted above, ask for permission before giving feedback. Something as simple as "May I offer a suggestion?" shows that you respect the person and their feelings. When giving feedback, make it objective and descriptive. Focus on specific behaviors and their consequences—never make it personal. And be sure to recognize and comment on positive behaviors and accomplishments, not just the negatives.

Follow-up. Coaching is most effective when there's a shared commitment on the part of both parties. Work together to agree on an action plan and schedule a follow-up meeting to evaluate progress. Hustad suggests using questions like "How are we going to begin?", "When will that be completed?", and "May I hold you responsible for . . . ?" Make it clear that you'll be available to provide support or answer questions—then make sure that you are.

instance, may actually be a heightened sensitivity to others—and could be very valuable in sales, customer service, or consulting.

Don't Leave Your Objectivity Behind

Careful observation and assessment are critical to effective—and fair—coaching. Feedback should be linked to specific examples, not vague or general impressions. Flaherty suggests that coaches ask themselves the following, "Is the assessment based upon observations that can be made by any competent observer, and is the coach able to cite particular instances of the observation?" Before jumping to solutions, make sure that you've seen enough to draw an accurate conclusion. If necessary, check your assessment with other trusted colleagues.

Be Fully Present

In any coaching situation—whether it's an informal encounter or a formal performance review—focus all of your attention on the other person. Notes Hustad, "Many managers are so used to multi-tasking and juggling projects that they're often unaware of just how distracted and fragmented their personal presence really is." Don't shuffle through papers, read your mail, think about your golf game or what you'll have for lunch.

Look at the person, not your computer screen. And listen actively, noting not just the words but the emotions behind them and the unspoken messages.

Build Self-management Skills in Your People

Besides trying to enhance performance, good coaches nurture the self-perception and growth of their people. The goal here is to develop in each person the capacity for self-awareness and self-knowledge that over time leads to self-correction. Explains Flaherty, "Well-coached clients can observe when they are performing well and when they are not and will make any necessary adjustments independently of the coach." In other words, the best coaches aim to make themselves unnecessary and obsolete.

Great coaches know that if they focus on getting the most out of their people, the bottom line will take care of itself. Why? Because people who feel valued and respected stick around, rewarding you with love, loyalty, and hard work. They're willing to go the extra mile because you've taken the time to help them get more out of work—and life. "Be the coach who tells them you believe in them," says White. "Then step back and watch what happens."

So what can you do with Frank? First you have to gain

his permission to enter into a coaching relationship, and then you have to build trust. So begin by looking for the coachable moments. He's probably feeling embattled; he already knows he's not as creative as the others. The direct approach may be the best. Catch him after one of those not-so-successful brainstorming sessions. Don't confront him immediately after he grants you his permission—instead, tell him you'll be looking for opportunities in the days ahead when the two of you can talk productively, when events are fresh in your minds.

Then, build some trust by starting with his strengths. He's a great researcher and makes a good devil's advocate. Perhaps you could take one of his devilish comments—which the rest of the group experiences as a roadblock to creativity—and use it to launch the group into a new round of brainstorming. ("Wait—Frank's concerns about legal impediments make sense. How could we address those and still generate all those new options? Frank, in the meantime, could you generate a history of legal decisions that relate to this area of consumer behavior?")

Or perhaps you could put Frank's two strengths together and have him provide the rest of the team with historical evidence of successes and failures in each new area of product development. That effort could help the other team members focus on the most promising niches and allow them to be more productive. ("Frank, I hear what you're saying about online options never succeeding with that demographic. Historically, what services have succeeded?") This way Frank will become creative without even being aware of it.

Redefine his role as the team historian, and you might even be able to get his productivity measured along different lines. Get him to research and write his reports throughout the product development process and across all the various team efforts. That way, the rest of the team can focus on being creative. And, at the very least, within the team it will be clear that what he's doing does add to the overall team effort.

Finally, look for ways to get Frank to monitor his own behavior. If you make him responsible for only playing devil's advocate once initial brainstorming is completed, for example, he will begin to see his role in the team as less adversarial and more productive.

For Further Reading

Coaching: Evoking Excellence in Others by James Flaherty (1999, Butterworth-Heinemann)

Drive Your People Wild Without Driving Them Crazy by Jennifer White (2001, Capstone Publishing)

Reprint C0112D

Employee Recognition and Reward with Bob Nelson

* * *

In this economic climate, it is more critical than ever to make your staff feel recognized for their contributions. *Harvard Management Update* sought the advice of best-selling author and employee motivation expert Bob Nelson, who has worked with such companies as FedEx, Time Warner, and IBM, on how to best handle this.

What's so important about informal, manager-initiated recognition?

It's important because recognition is about feeling special, and more times than not, it is hard to feel special from a corporate program where everyone gets the same thing, like a five-year pin. To be effective, recognition needs to come from those we hold in high esteem, such as one's manager.

What is necessary for delivering effective informal recognition?

Timing is important. The sooner you acknowledge employees' performance, the clearer they get the message, the more likely they are to repeat the desired performance.

Recognition is most powerful when it's contingent. Companies will bring in doughnuts on Friday and give people cards on their birthday, and all of a sudden you've got an entitlement culture. If you do stuff just to be nice, people end up expecting more. So make recognition contingent upon desired behavior and performance; they'll value the recogntion more and you'll get better results.

And you have got to keep it fresh, relevant, and sincere. Any incentive has less punch with repeated use.

What kinds of recognition and rewards do employees want most?

I conducted an Internet survey that gave people choices of 52 items. The No. 1 factor they valued was "managerial support and involvement"—asking employees their opinions, involving them in decisions, giving them authority to do their jobs, supporting them when they make a mistake, and so forth. Also important were flexible working hours, learning and development opportunities, manager availability, and time.

Employees also want basic praise. In the top 10 factors, there were four types of praise: personal praise, written praise, public praise, and electronic praise. Those are the hottest ones for people, and none of them costs a dime!

How do you choose what type of praise to use in a given situation?

Weigh these factors:

- Availability of the medium: How often do you actually see the individual—do you manage him from a distance or does he telecommute? Do you have occasion for public praise such as periodic staff meetings?

- Employee preference: Do you know how the employee prefers to be praised—have you ever discussed it with her? For example, an introverted employee would likely prefer a written or electronic note versus public recognition.

- Manager comfort zone: What forms of praise are you comfortable giving? If you feel awkward giving face-to-face praise, for example, you probably won't do it even if you feel you should. If you are uncomfortable speaking publicly, it might be better to skip public praise for something that is more personal and sincere.

Are there special considerations to delivering recognition in tough economic conditions?

Yes. The times when we need to do it the most, we tend to do it least. Say you give a team award that used to come with $250 but because you can't afford the $250, you stop giving the team award anymore. I say still give the team award. Say something like, "We've had to drop the financial aspect to hunker down, but it doesn't diminish the value of the job that this team did, especially at this time." When we are up against it, just a word of support, a team lunch, a "hang in there," can go a very long way.

For Further Reading

Make Their Day! Employee Recognition That Works by Cindy Ventrice (2003, Berrett-Koehler)

The Magic of Employee Recognition: 10 Proven Tactics from CalPERS and Disney by Dee Hansford (2003, Worldat-Work)

Other People's Habits: How to Use Positive Reinforcement to Bring Out the Best in People Around You by Aubrey C. Daniels (2000, McGraw-Hill)

Reprint U0309D

Real Empowerment? Manage the Boundaries

• • •

Alan Randolph

The best-run companies routinely beat the competition by turning responsibility and ownership inside out. The traditional model of management was *external control:* someone else defined employees' tasks, goals, and behaviors, and someone else assessed their performance. The new model might be called *internal control:* employees themselves take responsibility for this work. Trouble is, most managers and employees don't know how to make the shift, and they're usually afraid to try. Managers fear loss of control. Employees fear being held accountable for failure.

But it can be done. A successful shift to internal control relies, paradoxically, on managers making effective use of boundaries, that is, the limits on what people are expected to do. There are four keys:

View boundaries as rubber bands.

In traditional organizations, boundaries tell people what they can't do. They're like barbed wire, designed to keep people under control. But boundaries can also be seen as elastic, stretching to fit the degree of autonomy for which people are prepared and ready. In an Australian manufacturing company, for example, teams on the shop floor were initially given narrow boundaries. They were allowed to make decisions only regarding less-complex tasks such as safety, housekeeping, or measuring quality. Over time the teams became more accustomed to responsibility, and so took on tasks such as selecting work methods, assigning daily jobs, and contacting external customers. Motivation soared and results were outstanding.

Watch the process closely—
it isn't predictable.

The shift to internal control is an artful, often unpredictable process. Sometimes teams are ready for wider boundaries before managers expect it, and it's essential that managers seize the opportunities to stretch the boundaries. Consider the experience of a U.S. distribution company that was facing significant budget cuts. Team members who had already gained some experience with autonomous operation were asked to come up with cuts totalling 4%. They generated an abundance of ideas within this boundary, such as cutting down on overnight shipments. But they also produced many ideas for raising revenues, such as contacting customers to ensure receipt of a shipment and to see if the customer needed anything else. Managers, to their credit, reacted positively to this stretching of the boundary.

Expect discouragement.

The third key is an interesting paradox: when discouragement sets in—and it will—people are usually ready for more responsibility than they realize. The smart move is to praise the progress, then widen the boundaries a little more. Employees want to take on more responsibility, but often they're afraid to do so. By widening the boundaries a little, you let them know that you believe in their ability to rise to the challenge. A company in the utility industry, for instance, reacted to discouragement by asking employees to begin defining and working toward performance-improvement goals for their teams. At first the teams resisted, offering few suggestions. But the team leaders stood firm, acknowledging each suggestion that trickled in and encouraging people to produce more. Gradually the number of ideas began to increase. Eventually one team was able to implement a suggestion regarding salvage of parts that resulted in savings of more than $100,000 in less than three months.

Define the context.

Ultimately, the continuous expansion of boundaries means that external boundaries will seem to disappear. In fact, the boundaries are still there; they're just inside people's heads. But effective *internal* control has to be based on clear values, perspective, and direction, and setting those is management's job. A midwestern food company, for example, eliminated traditional organizational functions such as personnel, finance, and engineering, and gave those duties to teams. But the company's management had taken pains to establish a set of values and strategic priorities, so the teams were able to make budget decisions and solve their problems within these parameters. The teams held themselves accountable for results and held individual members responsible for their contributions.

Can your organization achieve this kind of autonomy? Of course. You just have to be willing to give up control by widening boundaries. These four keys will help you release the power in people—if you're willing to take the risk.

Reprint U0007D

Match Techniques to Employee Types

• • •

Different groups of employees—managers, women, older workers, younger workers—have unique forms of value to offer and distinctive interests that they weigh while making career choices. To capture their value and win the loyalty of the best among these groups, you'll need to adapt your retention and engagement strategies accordingly.

The following selections show you how to do just that. For example, to retain your best managers, watch for and address signs of burnout promptly. This insidious condition is particularly common among overburdened managers. To reverse the "brain drain" that occurs if talented female workers encounter barriers to advancement, make sure women participate in important business interactions—such as informal business networking, mentoring relationships, and socializing with clients. Additional selections explain how to hang on to older workers (known for their reliability and productivity) and younger employees (many of whom can offer fresh perspectives and an entrepreneurial spirit).

Keys to Retaining Your Best Managers in a Tight Job Market

• • •

Marie Gendron

A roundup of recent labor market studies leads to just one conclusion: the job market has never been hotter for managers and other senior executives. As a result, the issue of retaining key employees has taken on paramount importance in virtually every American company.

"The economy is wonderfully strong," says Vincent Webb, vice president of marketing at Management Recruiters International Inc. (MRI). "And companies are

117

catching up on maybe some overreaction in management job cuts in 1991 and 1992. We're seeing a dearth of middle managers. But the real thing driving this is just good growth in the economy and strong demand for goods and services." The latest hiring survey conducted by MRI reveals that companies nationwide plan to add management staff at a record rate in the first half of 1998. Of the nearly 4,300 executives surveyed in MRI's 16th annual study, fully 56% plan to increase their mid- to upper-management and professional staffs.

With the demand for staff booming, companies are finding it harder than ever to hold onto the talented managers—and future managers—already on the payroll. "There's a lot of poaching going on and a lot of effort to try to get people from other companies," says Steve Collins, editor of the newsletters *Consultants News* and *Executive Recruiter News*. "Companies are having a hard time keeping people because they do get all kinds of offers."

Foreseeing a red-hot job market, the Society for Human Resources Management (SHRM) polled its members last year about the greatest threats they saw to retention. The results highlight four key areas that firms should watch closely: salaries, advancement opportunities, making employees feel appreciated, and burnout.

Competitive Salaries

Not surprisingly, the single greatest threat, cited by 89% of the SHRM respondents, was higher salaries offered by other organizations. "The good news is, the biggest factor is the easiest one to fix," says Barry Lawrence, SHRM's spokesman. "Figure out what your region is offering. If you want to keep people, you're going to have to pay competitive salaries."

Companies seeking to retain workers should not look just at the pay level in their industry, they should also examine internal pay disparities—in other words, how pay for each job compares to similar jobs within the organization. The easiest way to get industry salary comparisons is to hire one of the big management consulting firms. But companies can get the same information more cheaply, says Lawrence, by simply tracking classified ads on the Internet, by networking with members of human resources organizations, or by approaching trade organizations.

Paying competitive salaries does not necessarily mean you have to out-spend all of your competitors. "In some areas of information technology, pay is a big issue and people can change jobs twice a year and get double-digit pay increases," says Webb. "But in most cases, people are looking for a better culture in which to be, a better match. Most people aren't looking for double-digit increases in pay. But the bar is higher today in terms of participation in equity with the company. Employees should have a chance to share in the success of the company if it grows."

Robust Career Advancement Opportunities

Employee dissatisfaction with career advancement opportunities within the company was listed as a threat to retention by 85% of the SHRM survey respondents. "People want to grow professionally in their career," Lawrence observes. "It's also important in this day and age because we don't have that sort of paternal relationship [in which employees have a job for life]."

This year, Texas Instruments (TI) made improving individual development one of its top three business priorities for the second year in a row. Accordingly, every one of the company's 40,000 workers must have a personal development plan in place for the coming year. The idea behind the mandate, explains Tegwin Pulley, TI's director of diversity and staffing services, is "to have every employee be focused on being the best they can be. People are happy when they're the best they can be and they're productive." Personal development plans are created by employees and then reviewed by their managers, who ensure that the company provides the training or education the employees need to meet their goals. For example, TI provides extensive in-house training and also picks up the full tab for employees taking higher-education classes.

Focus groups indicate that these programs are already paying dividends in terms of positive employee attitudes about their jobs and the company. Grassroots employee groups—comprising African-American employees, female employees, and parents—are also having an effect. Such groups meet to discuss career and other on-the-job issues, but they also perform community service in the neighborhoods where members work. "They're not feel-good programs," Pulley emphasizes, "they're productivity programs that make people feel that TI is a great place to work."

Your company may lack the resources of a Texas Instruments, but you can still help employees advance their careers and feel good about their employer. Many companies get hung up by restricting pay raises to particular job levels, short-changing workers who are doing good work but may not yet have made vice president. Other companies are achieving improved results, Lawrence points out, by doing away with formal titles and rewarding workers financially for developing particular skills rather than for simply moving up through the hierarchy.

Making Employees Feel Appreciated

Feeling underappreciated was the third largest threat to retention, said SHRM members. This concern can be addressed without expending any financial resources at all, and it is also an area in which middle managers can make all the difference in whether workers stay or leave. Workers need to know how they're doing more often than once a year at their formal performance appraisal meeting. It's as important to tell them when they're doing well as it is to point out when they screw up.

"You have to have a continuous performance appraisal system," Lawrence continues. "That means just talking with your people and giving them feedback about how they're doing. It's really so simple and we don't always take the time to do it."

To ensure that managers are giving continuous feedback to their subordinates, many companies are now requiring such communication as part of the managers' pay. Managers who are not used to talking to their workers regularly may need additional training in communication, but the investment is usually well worth it.

Burnout

A big factor warring against retention, according to the SHRM survey: employees who are overworked and burned out. Ironically, some of the burnout is among workers doing double-time because it takes so long to find and hire quality new employees in this overheated job market.

The solution, Lawrence suggests, is for line managers to work closely with the human resources department and upper management to create a long-term, strategic staffing plan that ensures there are enough people—and the right people—to do the job. "With virtually zero unemployment, it's really hard," he says. "Some of this is not entirely within a manager's control, but you have to do the best you can. One thing companies are trying to do is realize that they may not be able to get the best person they want, but they can get the second best and bring this person up to speed. To do that, you need to know ahead of time what your needs are going to be so you can do the training. You have limited resources and limited time, so you'd better be using them effectively."

In departments that are short-handed because the company is pinching every penny in order to compete, managers need to be very strategic about what they ask their workers to do. Every task should be considered in light of whether it adds value to the customer—if it doesn't, eliminate it.

A company that has recently downsized, or one that plans to downsize in the future, can have an especially hard time retaining the workers it wants to keep. The career services firm Lee Hecht Harrison recently released a report called "Beyond Downsizing: Staffing and

Workforce Management for the Millennium," for which it interviewed more than 500 companies. The report found that in the wake of a decade of costly and stressful corporate downsizings, successful organizations are employing six strategies to get the most from their workers and retain talented employees.

A MORE DISCIPLINED EMPLOYEE SELECTION PROCESS. Leading-edge organizations develop clear descriptions of each job that needs to be filled, how those jobs might evolve, and what type of person is needed to fill each position.

COACHING RATHER THAN COMMANDING EMPLOYEES. This "guide, don't dictate" approach enables managers to take on more subordinates, creates a more flexible workforce by giving employees the tools to be self-reliant, and enhances employee job satisfaction by encouraging greater individual responsibility.

BROADENING THE DISCUSSION. Employees at cutting-edge organizations are being asked to assume greater responsibility for the company's performance, so it's more critical than ever that they have adequate information about corporate vision, strategies, and objectives.

EXPANDING CAREER DEVELOPMENT OPTIONS. Take a cue from Texas Instruments: help employees develop the skills they need to move ahead within the organization.

INTERNAL REDEPLOYMENT OF PERSONNEL. This allows organizations to gain greater flexibility while retaining top employees through times of change and shifting resource needs.

FLEXIBLE WORK ARRANGEMENTS. In the SHRM survey, 71% of the respondents said employees leave because of difficulty balancing work and personal life. Offering flexible work arrangements doesn't mean every employee has to be a telecommuter. It could mean early start times or compressed work weeks (where, for example, employees work four ten-hour days). Job sharing and part-time opportunities can also help companies retain valuable employees whose personal situations have changed since they came on board as full-timers.

The key to these arrangements: make them available to *all* employees who can prove that their proposed schedule change will not hurt the company. Limiting the programs to employees with young children breeds resentment because workers could have any number of reasons for wanting a flexible schedule—from caring for ailing parents to training for a marathon. The company should never put itself in the position of judging the personal merit of an employee's request.

"Not to be too flowery, but retention is a tapestry. All kinds of things go into it," says Stephen Harrison, president of Lee Hecht Harrison, which is a wholly owned subsidiary of Adecco. "Unless the approach you use is an integrated one, forget the prospect of success in retention strategies. There is little room for rifle shots—such as, 'Oh my gosh, we need to enhance our 10-year goldwatch program.' Rifle shots have little effect in the current job market."

If, despite your company's best efforts, an employee does decide to leave, that worker can still provide insights useful to future retention efforts. Always do a thorough exit interview with every departing worker. "It's a wonderful opportunity to get experiential data," says Lawrence. "People who are leaving tend to be freer with their thoughts than regular employees. You have to take it with a grain of salt, of course, because they may have an ax to grind. But it's valuable information."

For Further Reading

The AMA Handbook for Employee Recruitment and Retention by Mary F. Cook, editor, and Nary Cook (1992, AMACOM)

"Beyond Downsizing: Staffing & Workforce Management for the Millennium" (1998, Lee Hecht Harrison)

"Society for Human Resources Management Retention Practices Survey and White Paper" (1997, SHRM)

Reprint U9806A

Why Women Leave—And What Corporations Can Do About It

• • •

Kristen B. Donahue

Women are leaving corporate America at twice the rate of men. Should companies be alarmed by this trend? And is there anything they can do?

Yes to both, current thinking suggests. Just-published research by the National Foundation of Women Business Owners (NFWBO), provides new data about why women are trading the corporate world for the entrepreneurial frontier. Mary Mattis, vice president of research and advisory services for Catalyst, a nonprofit firm that assisted with the study, says the findings should be regarded as a "wake-up call for those who seek to retain entrepreneurial women."

The study, called *Paths to Entrepreneurship—New Directions for Women in Business*, was released at a conference sponsored by Simmons Graduate School of Management. It found that the primary reason women started their own businesses was the desire to do for themselves what they had been doing for their employers. Another strong impetus was the inspiration of a winning business concept: roughly half of the women surveyed were motivated by the combination of hitting upon a great idea and identifying a market niche. A third major reason was the desire for more flexibility.

"There's no such thing as a glass ceiling—there's just a very dense layer of men," quipped Eileen M. Friars, president of NationsBank Card Services, at the Simmons conference. Joking aside, one-fourth of the women surveyed considered the glass ceiling a very real barrier to advancement—an increase of some 250% from two decades ago. Mattis's explanation? Women's higher expectations of what is now possible in the business world: "They do not expect to be fighting the same battles that were fought by women 20 years ago."

The Resulting Brain Drain

Companies are feeling the pain of the exodus of women executives. In addition to the loss of intellectual capital, the costs include negative effects on staff morale and the cost of finding replacements. And let's not forget competition: women who have founded their own businesses within the past ten years are more likely to start an enterprise that is directly related to their previous experience. Thus, corporations face the very real threat of competition from these women.

How Companies Can Respond

In *Women Breaking Through: Overcoming the Final 10 Obstacles at Work,* Deborah J. Swiss notes that identifying gender equity as a legitimate business concern is the first step in the process, but organizations "cannot create a new structure that whole-heartedly includes women without first identifying the fundamental flaws in the old ways of conducting business—flaws that trail women from their first job interview to the day they enter the corporate board room." Similarly, the *Paths to Entrepreneurship* study indicated that a number of women could be enticed back into the corporate world by more rewards for and recognition of the contributions of women, as well as by more flexible work arrangements.

The following measures will foster a more hospitable workplace not only for women, but for all employees.

Analyze the current situation.

The *Paths to Entrepreneurship* research findings did not surprise Ellen Gabriel, national director for the advancement of women at Deloitte & Touche LLP, who did similar research within her firm five years ago when it became apparent that the large numbers of women leaving the firm were not going home to have babies as assumed, but were in fact remaining in the workforce or starting their own businesses. "You need to identify how many women are in upper management positions, and how many women are in the pipelines, positioned for future advancement," she advises. "Then go out and talk to those women, find out what's important to them." Such conversations prompted Deloitte & Touche to offer more flexible work arrangements and to launch programs to help its women managers advance in their careers.

Facilitate discussion and exploration of gender equity issues.

A host of factors influence promotion: gender-based stereotypes; an absence of female role models; an absence of objective performance standards; and the exclusion of women from male-only traditions, including informal business networks, mentoring opportunities, and after-hours socializing with clients. "Critical to career momentum," writes Swiss, "these informal channels for relationship building and business communication are fully accessible to most men but quietly unwelcoming to most women."

Discussing workplace equality can be painful. Some men may feel threatened, others angry; some women may clam up for fear of reprisal if they speak out. At Deloitte & Touche, says Gabriel, "a two-day 'gender awareness' workshop is now mandatoryfor every management employee. The purpose is to provide a common language for discussing gender-related issues. The issues are removed from the sphere of individual personalities, and are discussed from a business point of view."

Eradicate "invisible" barriers to women's success.

A nice idea, you might be thinking—let's also wipe out world hunger while we're at it.

Exactly how does one go about breaking down invisible barriers? If you're serious about attracting and retaining top women, then take a long, hard look at your corporate environment. The barriers are real but subtle, notes Gabriel, adding that they have "a lot to do with male-dominated hierarchies and perceptions and stereotypes that can influence all kinds of decisions. We need to raise awareness of these perceptions, and force organizations to come to grips with them."

Swiss stresses that firms must be proactive in identifying high-potential women and giving them equal access to career-enhancing opportunities: line positions, skill-building opportunities, special project assignments, appointment to high-visibility teams, and committee and project leadership. And don't assume that because a woman is of childbearing age, she must be on the "mommy track." "Until workplace standards become gender-blind," writes Swiss, companies need to "support nontraditional forums for a woman's career development: sponsorship in community organizations, nomination to business and nonprofit boards, membership in women's business groups." These affiliations not only connect women with peers and potential mentors from other organizations—they broaden the company's client base as well.

Genuinely open job searches are also critical. "Staff search committees with people who will identify the broadest possible candidate base," Swiss advises, "uncovering nontraditional sources for nominees via community groups, nonprofit boards, and professional organizations whose memberships represent today's labor pool."

Get support wherever you can.

Attempts to effect the changes outlined above will fall flat without active support coming from all levels of the organization. Some suggestions:

Hold supervisors responsible for meeting gender equity goals. Swiss cautions against linking a manager's compensation to a quota system, but instead says that "a manager should be rewarded for fostering a climate where women flood the applicant pools and move up the ranks at the same rate as their male peers."

Adopt interim measures. In-house women's groups, with the sanction of top management, can help "demonstrate the link between gender equity and the bottom line," says Swiss. An ombudsperson, reporting directly to a senior executive, can handle bias incidents and sexual harassment allegations while serving as an advocate for organizational change.

Send a message from the top. Communication from senior management, notes Swiss, "signals a new business agenda where women enjoy the freedom to make unencumbered career decisions, where the organization accepts a broader range of leadership styles, and where the very best talent rises."

Promote the understanding that women's ways of managing are good for business.

Many older books on management advise that women who want to succeed in business should act as much like men as possible. But such advice gives the impression that women offer no unique positive benefits to the corporate world. Today there is a wealth of research to the contrary. In her book *The Female Advantage: Women's Way of Leadership,* Sally Helgesen conducted "diary studies" of women leaders, documenting how they made decisions, scheduled their days, gathered and dispersed information, motivated others, delegated tasks, and structured their companies. She found that many organizations run by women are based not on a hierarchical pyramid, but instead resemble a web in which leaders reach out, not down, to the rest of the organization, creating communities that rely on information sharing. Moreover, 76% of the women in the *Paths to Entrepreneurship* survey offered at least one policy or practice that was consciously different from those of their former organizations. Regardless of firm size, the women entrepreneurs reported that offering more flexibility, understanding, and a more open management style were key differences in their companies' modus operandi.

What's notable is that many aspects of this so-called female approach to management have entered the mainstream and are being implemented by male and female managers alike. In today's economy, information is replacing authority as the key to successful management. Women are demonstrating that they are naturally inclined to manage in ways that foster and improve this flow of information.

For Further Reading

The Female Advantage: Women's Ways of Leadership by Sally Helgesen (1995, Currency Doubleday)

Paths to Entrepreneurship—New Directions for Women in Business (1998, The National Foundation for Women Business Owners)

Women Breaking Through: Overcoming the Final 10 Obstacles at Work by Deborah J. Swiss (1997, Peterson's/Pacesetter Books)

Reprint U9806C

Managing the Labor Shortage: Part 1

How to Keep Your 50-Somethings

• • •

This is the age of human capital—and of tight labor markets. Companies have finally realized that competitive advantage resides mostly in people, and that finding and keeping good managers and employees is a strategic necessity. But how do you attract and retain the best and brightest when the competition for people is so brutal?

To make matters worse, two demographic time bombs are quietly ticking away. The baby boom generation—nearly half the workforce—is growing older, and many boomers have no intention of sticking around doing the same job till they turn 65. Yet the age cohort right behind the boomers is one of the smallest ever, and so can't begin to pick up the demographic slack. Result:

finding and keeping good people will be even tougher in the future. Take a good look at today's acute shortages in IT departments, advises Jerry McAdams, a consultant with Watson Wyatt Worldwide—because that's what your whole company will be facing tomorrow.

What to do? One key is to confront the age-cohort issue head-on. This article discusses tools and techniques for retaining—and getting the best out of—the aging boomers.

Baby boomers, it is estimated, are now turning 50 at the rate of 11,000 a day, or close to one every seven seconds.

So what? Managers in the past would have yawned at the news—or rejoiced. Fifty-year-olds, after all, were among a company's most reliable and productive employees. They enjoyed the perks of career advancement and seniority. Most expected to stick around another 15 years.

But today's fiftyish employees are in less satisfying circumstances. Their prospects for promotion are limited—too many people, not nearly enough senior slots. Most are uncertain about their job security; few will get much of a pension. Some are already setting their sights on early retirement, a second career, or a better job somewhere else. Some will get sick or injured—or will leave to care for an aging parent—and never return. Others will feel they must stay on for financial reasons, however frustrated and disgruntled they may be.

Let this situation fester, and over time your company

will lose many of these people. (It will keep only the ones who can't think of anything better to do.) That's a problem, in part because whole plants or departments may be decimated. "Many employers have large groups in this category," warns Glenn L. Dalton, a principal for Sibson & Co. "And there's a domino effect. One leaves, and another says, 'Hey, I'm out of here too.' Next thing you know, half the electricians in your maintenance department are gone." McAdams adds that the boomers aren't just numerous, they're also critically important to most companies. If they leave, most of your organization's intellectual capital walks out the door.

As yet, few companies have faced up to the problem of an aging baby-boom cohort. But a handful of HR specialists have begun to think and write about it, and their recommendations are similar. If you want to keep the boomers on the payroll and productive, they say, you can—but you may have to create a workplace in which conventional assumptions about job descriptions, hours, pay, benefits, and so on go out the window.

Open the Conversation

Step one in this process—no surprise—is to begin talking with employees in this age cohort. Companies "need to look at boomers almost as a diversity group," says Richard Pimentel, a partner in the consulting firm Milt Wright & Associates. "This is a big chunk of the population, and things are changing for them. Who are they?

What are their needs?" Just starting the dialogue may open fruitful avenues for exploration. Does your company's medical coverage meet this group's needs? Would they value long-term-care insurance? "Keeping boomers happy isn't just a matter of a raise every year," says Pimentel. "Companies have to be creative."

The Key: Flexibility

Flexible benefit plans are a no-brainer, but the flexibility principle extends to other areas as well. Hours, for instance. Life seems shorter at 50-plus; many employees at this age don't want to work even 40 hours a week, let alone 60. They do want to work part-time, to share jobs, to telecommute. They're interested in sabbaticals, unpaid time off, released time for community projects. They like flexible schedules. "Phased retirement," allowing employees to reduce their hours in stages, may grow more popular, says Martha Edwards, multimedia director for Age Wave Communications.

More Interesting Work

While they're on the job, surveys show, baby boomers want autonomy, a sense of meaning, and a chance to learn new things. That, say several experts, means redesigning the way tasks get done. Let people work on their own. Teach the basics of business; help people understand how their job contributes to company performance. Give them a chance to take on new challenges and pick up new skills—but don't assume everyone will get up to speed without help. "You have to make a conscious investment in training for a more mature workforce," says Mark Francis, a vice president at Age Wave, "particularly in the technology area. But it will be money well spent."

Tailor Your Compensation System

Companies have traditionally relied on one-size-fits-all pay plans. Those, too, may have to give way, says Sibson & Co.'s Dalton. Younger employees want cash. Older ones may prefer larger contributions to a retirement fund. One change many companies will be looking at: a big increase in variable-pay percentages, from 5% or 10% of salary to (in Jerry McAdams's view) 20%, 30%, or even higher. What's the importance of variable pay? It's a perfect fit with boomer attitudes, explains Roger Herman, CEO of the Herman Group. "I want autonomy, I want to be in charge of my own destiny. If you give me a position where I can influence the amount of money I earn, now you've got my attention."

Creating so flexible a workplace won't be easy. But the alternative—standing by while your 50-somethings pick up and leave—may damage your company beyond repair.

Reprint U9909A

Managing the Labor Shortage: Part 2

Finding—and Keeping— Good Young Employees

• • •

Nobody can find enough young workers these days. This should be no surprise: labor markets are tight everywhere, and the post–Baby Boom age cohort ("Generation X") is remarkably small. The absolute number of workers aged 25 to 34 has declined about 12% since 1990 and will continue to fall for several more years.

So what are companies doing to cope with this scarcity? Some focus on new recruitment and retention strategies. Others outsource or automate jobs once done by entry-level employees. A few companies, desperate for help, are hiring people they once wouldn't have let in the door. These moves may help. But there's an opportunity here to do more than respond on an ad-hoc basis, say consultants in the field. The savviest managers are solving their staffing problems with a systemic approach—in effect, by reinventing their notions of what constitutes a job and what constitutes a workplace.

To determine the right mix of strategies for your company, consider the options:

Recruitment

The new approach to recruitment is partly a matter of tactics. Managers and HR staffers are learning to comb online employment sites and are stepping up on-campus efforts. They pay referral bonuses to employees who recommend new hires. "Some companies are actually making acquisitions just to get talent," says John Parkington, a principal in Watson Wyatt Worldwide's San Francisco office. "That lets them bring in a team of 10 or 15 people all at once."

But behind the new tactics is a different way of thinking: instead of just interviewing people, companies are developing recruitment programs that look for all the world like product-marketing strategies. These companies develop "value propositions" designed to differentiate the company as an employer from its competitors. They segment the market of prospective employees, identifying target groups and crafting unique employment opportunities. (An insurance company—cited by David S. Friedman in a recent issue of the *McKinsey Quarterly*—hires schoolteachers to sell policies during their summer vacations. Though most go back to teaching in the fall, a few quit each year and become permanent sales reps.) To land their prospects, companies assemble customized compensation packages, often including signing bonuses and stock options.

Retention

Keeping new hires is a particular challenge with Gen-X workers, who are notoriously mobile. So companies have instituted "staying" bonuses and lucrative incentive plans with multiyear vesting schedules. They have also added unusual benefits: for example, CACI International offers its employees auto insurance, home insurance, and prepaid legal services as well as health coverage.

Recently, some employers have created a position known as retention manager, responsible for doing anything possible to reduce turnover. One emphasis: mapping out short-term career paths that provide variety and challenge to young employees. Another: helping interpersonally challenged managers learn not to alienate new staffers. No one who hates his or her boss is likely to stay long regardless of the money.

Automation and Outsourcing

Bank tellers and gas-station attendants are vanishing breeds. McDonald's Corp. recently announced that it is testing computerized order-taking kiosks. More and more of the work once done by entry-level employees is being automated or made more efficient through technology. And more work is starting to be farmed out. Software companies, unable to find enough young American engineers, outsource the writing of code to programmers overseas. In health care, notes Friedman,

Enlarging the Entry-level Pool

Big companies could once be choosy about the young employees they hired. No more. Today, employers needing large numbers of entry-level workers are drawing on demographic groups they once would have scorned. High-school dropouts. Former welfare recipients. People with disabilities who have never held a job. The catch: companies hiring these "nontraditional" workers often take on a double training obligation. Along with job skills, they must teach the rules and expectations governing the workplace. If you're not coming in to work, call. If you have finished the task you were assigned, ask for something else to do.

Marriott Corp. and a few other employers have com-

"suppliers make up prepackaged surgery kits to take a task out of the hospital and free up time for hard-to-find operating-room staff."

At first glance, outsourcing of this sort seems only to relocate the staffing problem, not to solve it. But outsourcing expands the pool of available employees. Also, the outsource vendors are specialists: they can not only do the job more efficiently, they can make themselves employers of choice in a particular field. Friedman points to ServiceMaster, a cleaning company that "has pursued a people-based strategy committed to turning otherwise dead-end jobs into steps in a career path."

---

prehensive training programs for employees who are new to the workforce. Others are hiring consultants such as Richard Pimentel of Milt Wright & Associates to teach them what to do. One key: helping supervisors learn patience and positive attitudes when dealing with nontraditional employees. Bullying and barking orders won't work, says Pimentel —the new hire may quit on the spot. Instead, supervisors need to learn coaching skills. Pimentel recommends they sit down with new people at the end of each day to go over problems and concerns.

"It means a couple of extra minutes for the supervisor," says Pimentel, "and they may say, 'I don't have those extra minutes.' But think about all the minutes they'll lose if that employee walks out the door."

Reinventing the Workplace

These three R's—recruitment, retention, and reorganization—can often provide a solution to the young-employee staffing crisis. But there's another way of approaching the situation, says Bruce Tulgan of Rainmaker Thinking, a consulting firm that has interviewed close to 10,000 young people over several years. Gen Xers are the quintessential free agents, flexible and entrepreneurial in their approach to work. So why do most employers persist in offering them conventional jobs? "Companies are always trying to fill positions on the org chart," declares Tulgan—"full-time, exclusive, on-site, uninterrupted jobs. But that's a very limited way of getting the work done."

Tulgan's solution: view the mercurial character of today's young-employee labor market as an opportunity, not a problem, and "get good at being fluid." If someone wants to work Monday through Wednesday and surf the rest of the week, cool—figure out how to arrange it. If someone else wants six months off to go to India, arrange that, too; let them "leave without leaving," and make provisions for them to return. Young employees who want flexible hours, telecommuting arrangements, consulting deals, or on-again, off-again work shouldn't be seen as problems or misfits. If your company can come up with a way of tapping into this talent pool, you'll be a step ahead of your competitors.

To be sure, says Tulgan, reinventing the workplace along these lines involves reassessing nearly everything about it—"recruitment, orientation, training, performance management, and rewards." Rather than investing a year in training new employees, for instance, put them to work right away and provide "just in time" training as their responsibilities increase. Tailor rewards more and more to individuals, less and less to salary scales—and tie them clearly to performance rather than seniority. (One high-tech company sets up project teams as almost-independent businesses, and pays team members a portion of the revenues they generate.) Every HR department—and probably every working manager—will have to maintain a talent bank of people who know the company and can deliver high-quality work.

A pain in the neck? Maybe. On the other hand, the double demographic crunch of tight labor markets and a shrinking pool of young workers is likely to be with us for a while. Companies can't afford to sit still.

Reprint U9910A

Extract Maximum Value from Employees

• • •

It's not enough to merely hang on to your talented workers; you also need to seize advantage of the unique knowledge, ideas, and skills that they bring to your workplace. When people see their talents being put to use in their organization, they feel appreciated. That emotion, in turn, engenders commitment to the organization.

In this section, you'll find articles explaining how to elicit valuable ideas from your employees. Often, "small" ideas that don't seem like much at first glance can make a big difference to your company's bottom line collectively—because rival companies can't easily recognize and copy them. Additional articles show you how to leverage workers' strengths while helping them improve weak areas, as well as how to capture the knowledge of employees who may ultimately move to other parts of your company (or other organizations all together).

Getting the Best Employee Ideas with Alan G. Robinson

• • •

The right approach to generating ideas from your employees creates a virtuous circle, say Alan G. Robinson and Dean M. Schroeder, professors at the University of Massachusetts Amherst and Valparaiso University, respectively. Workers become more engaged when they see their ideas being used. And managers, seeing the impact of employees' ideas, give employees more authority—which leads to more and better ideas.

How can you create such a win-win situation? Learn

to appreciate the power of small ideas, says Robinson, and throw out any beliefs about the need for financial incentives.

What's wrong with the typical approach to idea generation?

Ever since Frederick Taylor argued that management's job was to *think* and the worker's job to *do*, this has been most companies' default perspective. But, in fact, front-line workers have better knowledge of the particularities of products, services, and processes than managers do. They're better positioned to spot problems and opportunities.

What are some of the characteristics of an effective idea system?

Ideas are actively encouraged—from all quarters. Submitting ideas is simple, and the evaluation of suggestions is quick and effective. Pushing decision making down to the front lines for as many ideas as possible leads to better decisions, faster implementation, and lower processing costs; it also frees up managers' time.

Why the emphasis on small ideas?

Business leaders are always looking for the next breakthrough idea—the home run that will put them well ahead of the competition with one swing. Because of this, the systems and policies they put in place are aimed at big ideas.

Few managers realize how severely limiting this is. In many important aspects of business—customer service, responsiveness, quality, and managing costs—you just can't achieve excellence without getting the little things right.

At one of the bimonthly idea meetings at Grapevine Canyon Ranch in southwest Arizona, a housekeeper suggested creating special business card-sized pieces of paper with spaces for people to write their contact information. From faint imprints left on stacks of stationery in the rooms, the housekeeper had realized that many guests were using full sheets—the only writing paper provided—to swap names and addresses with other guests. This was both inconvenient for the guests and costly for the ranch.

This one idea didn't have a perceptible impact on performance or guest satisfaction. But taken together, all the small ideas make the ranch's service feel incredibly responsive.

What's more, most small ideas stay proprietary, whereas big ones don't. Big ideas are very visible to your competitors and are often countered or copied relatively easily. Because there's no natural way for competitors to find out about them, small ideas can add up to a huge competitive advantage.

How should companies guide idea generation?

A company's strategy should help it determine where to concentrate its search for ideas. Identifying the primary drivers of performance and then soliciting ideas related to those drivers—that's the ultimate alignment tool.

Do organizations need to reward ideas to guarantee a large flow of them?

Not as much as they think they do. The Japanese company Idemitsu gets more than a hundred ideas per employee each year without offering any bonuses. Besides, many seemingly commonsense reward plans—for instance, offering a percentage of the savings or profits from each idea—turn out to be counterproductive, creating an enormous amount of non-value-adding work and also undermining teamwork and trust.

Most employees have lots of ideas and would be thrilled to see them used. They take pride in contributing to the organization's success. So the most effective form of idea recognition is to implement the ideas rapidly and to give credit to the employees involved.

If you *do* want to offer financial rewards, base them on simple aggregate measures and distribute them to all employees, equitably and across the board.

For example, Kacey Fine Furniture links substantial quarterly employee bonuses to performance improvements such as reducing customer returns.

Reprint U0406E

Honing Strengths or Shoring Up Weaknesses

Which Is More Effective?

• • •

Melissa Raffoni

"You will excel only by maximizing your strengths, never by fixing your weaknesses," write Marcus Buckingham and Donald O. Clifton in their best-selling *Now, Discover Your Strengths*. The benefits of trying to improve upon often long-standing areas of weakness are marginal, they maintain. Besides, you don't need to have strength in every aspect of your role in order to be a standout. The implication for managers is that it's far more productive to exploit your direct reports' strengths to their fullest and to manage around their weaknesses.

As compelling as Buckingham and Clifton's argument is, the experts *Harvard Management Update* consulted suggest that it is too reductionistic. Although it seems natural to design work responsibilities so that you're playing to employees' particular strengths, you can't afford to have a single-minded focus on strengths.

> # An employee's motivation is often a more critical determinant of performance than her aptitude.

Ensuring that your company's needs are met often requires that you ask employees to address areas of weakness. What's more, "the underlying assumption, that people don't develop, is offensive," says Dr. Richard Boyatzis, chairman of the organizational behavior department at Case Western Reserve University's Weatherhead School of Management and coauthor, with Daniel Goleman and Annie McKee, of *Primal Leadership*. "Our research shows, time and time again, that people can and do change," he says. "Sustained change comes from balancing a focus on strengths and gaps—and keeping them in balance. If you don't stretch people, they will ultimately get bored with their jobs and leave."

Despite all the layoffs of the past year, it's still pretty difficult to recruit the most talented people. If the external searches don't pan out, executives must be able to develop people from within, transforming middling performers into world-class ones. To do this, start by identifying the skills and abilities that are the linchpins of your unit's success—regardless of whether they are your direct reports' strengths or weaknesses. Be strategic in your choice of weaknesses to concentrate on, customizing your approach to fit each individual's particular sources of motivation. And don't give the follow-through short shrift. Weaknesses, once identified, don't magically fix themselves; as a supervisor, you must partner with the employee to help the desired improvement come about.

A Strategic Approach to Addressing Weaknesses

Everybody has weaknesses and shortcomings—some of which, if not exactly intractable, seem stubbornly resistant to attempts at improvement over the decades. Although Sal Lanuto, CEO of JJ Wild, an IT solutions provider, acknowledges that there's no simple formula for determining how much time to spend helping an employee shore up a weakness, the key issue, he says, is to concentrate on "the weaknesses that matter."

Don't try to take on too much at once. Start with the flaws that prevent an employee from achieving minimal performance standards for key tasks. When you've taken care of those, move on to the weaknesses that are preventing him from advancing in his career.

A tipping-point analysis can be extremely helpful here. Instead of trying to get the employee to address his most glaring weaknesses, encourage him to develop competencies that, although not yet strengths, are close to "the level at which a relatively small improvement" or increase in the frequency of the competence will tip him "into outstanding performance," says Boyatzis.

In some instances, however, the law of diminishing returns will come into play: the effort required to close an individual's performance gap in a vital skill area will not be worth the time and cost. For example, says Lanuto, "we have had a really hard time making engineers into salespeople and vice versa. It's one thing to provide information that helps people better leverage their strengths; it's quite another to ask them to jump over the fence." A strategic approach to weaknesses pays big dividends here because it helps you recognize when it's time to consider workarounds.

If the employee's weaknesses persist but her strengths make her valuable to the company, try partnering or job sculpting, in which you tailor her job to create a better match between her responsibilities and her deep-seated life interests. "It's easier to look at all the things that need to be done, then be flexible in how you fit people into positions," says Nick Gaehde, president of Educators Publishing Service.

As you craft positions that play to individuals' strengths or better suit their needs, just remember that the company's needs come first. "Some crafting is typically in order, but not to the point where it doesn't help the company," says Timothy Butler, a psychologist, director of career development programs at Harvard Business School, and coauthor of *The 12 Bad Habits That Hold Good People Back*. "There may be a big mismatch between what the employee wants to do and what the company needs to get done." Adds Boyatzis: "Fitting people into roles works well in the short run, but not in the long run because it doesn't help to stretch and develop people—at least not the best leaders."

Customizing Your Managerial Interventions

Although the desire to treat people fairly is ingrained in managers, when it comes to motivating employees to address weaknesses—or to develop their strengths to the full potential, for that matter—you have to tailor your approach to fit the personality you're dealing with. This kind of customization doesn't have to be inequitable. "Managers often don't realize that it's OK to customize performance expectations to motivate different staff members," says Dr. Catherine Fitzgerald, a psychologist, executive coach, and coeditor of *Executive Coaching: Practices and Perspectives.* "On the other hand, if you ask parents how they deal with their children, they quickly realize the need to individualize their approach." So try to ascertain each report's primary sources of motivation—and don't assume that what motivates you will also motivate your direct reports, advises Holly Weeks, a communications consultant. You also need to take timing and context into account as you map out your pitch to a given employee. For example, "life or career changes," says Boyatzis, "can have a significant effect on motivation."

"People can make huge leaps and improve dramatically at any age," he continues. "They can change just as easily at 45 to 50 years old as when they're in their 20s. When they don't, it's typically because they don't want to—it's a motivational issue, not an impossible issue."

The whole notion of a strength can be misleading: an employee's motivation is often a more critical determinant of performance than her aptitude. "Some people have strengths that they are not inspired by," explains Fitzgerald. For example, an aptitude for math will be only marginally useful if the employee actually finds it boring. You have to do more than help employees discover their natural talents; you have to help them discern what energizes them most about work. Fitzgerald recommends that you ask the following questions about each of your direct reports: What does he love to do?

What sparks her interests? What worries her the most? What makes him a nervous wreck?

Employees' sources of energy and motivation aren't always readily apparent. Sometimes you have to do some prospecting to uncover them. "A big mistake many managers make is that they assume that people really know what they want and that it is just a matter of negotiation," says Butler. "The issue for most is that they do not know or are not able to really articulate what it takes to charge them up." Helping employees "think about what excites them and how it makes them better is good business. In our research, we found that the biggest determinant of people's satisfaction is the degree to which their fundamental interests are represented in their work."

Fortunately, human nature is on your side, says Butler. "As a general rule, people want to feel that they are growing and not being left by the wayside, and this often requires development in certain areas." Of course, says Boyatzis, you often need to "overemphasize strengths because people are bombarded with hearing about their weaknesses." But the crucial test comes when you need to motivate an employee to develop a weakness that he doesn't value.

"What people don't value, they neglect," says Weeks. "It's hard enough to motivate a person to cultivate a strength he doesn't value—imagine how much harder it would be to get him to cultivate a weakness that he doesn't value." And yet sometimes the company's needs dictate that you do just that.

How can you go about it? Emphasize to the employee

the strategic importance of shoring up the particular weakness. Describe the cost, to him, of continuing to neglect that ability. And minimize the pain as much as you can. Anything you can do to make the work on weaknesses less tedious will help, says Fitzgerald. "For example, if somebody is struggling with time management, and you know he's engaged by technology, try to find time-management tools he can use that might capture his imagination."

"What you don't want to do," says Butler, "is throw somebody into a sink-or-swim situation—most of us don't learn best that way."

For Further Reading

Now, Discover Your Strengths by Marcus Buckingham and Donald O. Clifton, Ph.D. (2001, Free Press)

Primal Leadership: Realizing the Power of Emotional Intelligence by Daniel Goleman, Richard Boyatzis, and Annie McKee (2002, Harvard Business School Press)

The 12 Bad Habits That Hold Good People Back: Overcoming the Behavior Patterns That Keep You from Getting Ahead by James Waldroop, Ph.D., and Timothy Butler, Ph.D. (2000, Currency)

Reprint U0206B

When Your Best People Leave, Will Their Knowledge Leave, Too?

• • •

David Boath and David Y. Smith

Executives often speak of their most important resource as the one that walks out the door each night. Yet few leaders are sufficiently guarding their organizations against the day when key people walk out the door for good. And with the rebounding economy, that day may be coming sooner than many firms would like to admit.

More so, as the workforce ages—and workers of all ages continue to be more transient—many companies are looking at an ongoing, irreplaceable loss of the knowledge, experience, and wisdom that have been a primary source of competitiveness and profitability.

That is, unless they begin to execute a strategic plan of action to retain and build on the great body of knowledge represented by their workforce. Such a plan should have the following goals:

- Help people capture and distribute knowledge— both their own and that of their coworkers.

- Support collaboration across time and space.

- Provide access to the learning and performance support needed to work most effectively.

- Implement organizational structures that lead to effective career development and succession planning.

The loss of knowledge and its effects on workforce productivity and performance represent a complex web of issues. It stands to reason, then, that no single or monolithic solution can address all the issues. Instead, organizations need to think in terms of a suite of strategies, techniques, and technologies. Companies seeking to pursue such an approach should follow these steps:

Identify the knowledge most at risk and institutionalize it.

Companies should begin by identifying where they are most at risk from the loss of information and experience. This involves, in part, establishing performance-management and career-development processes that carry with them the identification of employees who possess the most critical knowledge.

For example, as David W. De Long and Thomas O. Mann noted in "Stemming the Brain Drain" in Accenture's *Outlook Journal* (January 2003), "When air traffic dropped dramatically after September 11," Delta Air Lines cut the workforce to remain competitive. "So when 11,000 employees companywide agreed to take an early retirement or severance offer, Delta had less than two months to identify those employees who held jobs for which no backups or replacements had been trained . . . and then capture that knowledge before it walked out the door. Supervisors across the board worked with a team from Delta's learning services unit to narrow the list of 11,000 down to those veterans whose departure would represent a 'critical job loss.' Once these outstanding performers were identified, they were interviewed about their roles at the company. This way, Delta retained as much critical knowledge as possible on very short notice."

Establish more focused career-development and succession-planning programs.

A career-development program builds knowledge that professionals need to prepare for future roles. For example, following a recent fourfold increase in new-drug discoveries, Wyeth recognized that its 150 clinical study team leaders had become a mission-critical workforce among its 6,000 employees in research and development.

In an effort to retain and develop these increasingly important managers, the company developed a unique career-progression model that defined a set of critical competencies—as well as the required levels of profi-

> Don't lose the great body of knowledge represented by your workforce.

ciency—for each career level. It assessed all clinical study team leaders against those competencies and created individual development plans to address opportunities for improvement and growth. Wyeth also built tools to

Combating "Brain Drain"

Organizational knowledge loss is a systemic problem involving the entire employment life cycle: recruiting, hiring, performance, retention, and retirement. Companies may be tempted to implement a number of non-integrated solutions. While some of these—such as mentoring programs, knowledge databases, or hiring retirees as contractors—have some value, most are merely quick fixes, and comprehensive problems need comprehensive and integrated solutions.

Firms should implement the following to ensure they retain the expertise required to stay competitive:

- Workforce planning and organizational design, which ensures that structures and processes are in place to support career development, identification of most vital personnel, and succession planning.
- Workforce support and collaboration, using portal and enterprise resource management solutions.
- Learning design and delivery, focusing on anytime, anywhere learning and the powerful solutions found in today's performance simulation solutions.

enhance clinical study team leaders' knowledge further and established collaboration forums to allow continued learning and sharing of best practices.

Additionally, to help ensure that the organization's expertise in trial management continues to grow, clinical study team leaders join so-called capability teams, where they address process changes and training needs, and they are also now part of a new, centralized organization focused specifically on trial management.

Build knowledge communities.

In many organizations, knowledge resides solely with "experts," who take their knowledge with them when they leave. The right collaboration tools can capture experts' information and insights and help build a community around them, transforming their knowledge

> Organizational knowledge loss is a systemic problem involving the entire employment life cycle.

into community knowledge. One of the more seamless ways this can happen is by saving and archiving instant messaging (IM) conversations involving key company experts. Often filled with insight, these conversations are generally lost as soon as they disappear from computer screens. But new tools capture them and make them available for retrieval, thus ensuring that the knowledge transmitted through them remains in-house.

Adopt more advanced e-learning techniques, especially performance simulation.

E-learning has revolutionized workforce training. Freeing organizations from a restrictive belief that learning happens only when it's "officially" administered in classroom settings, e-learning has permitted a consistent distribution of high-quality content, enabling anytime, anywhere learning that is learner-driven.

Performance simulations, in particular, have proven to be highly effective learning techniques. Completing tasks in an environment that looks like the real thing—with rules-based feedback and remediation—provides insights, assessments and coaching. Learners are directed to expert "war stories" and perspectives, specific reference materials, industry best practices, and practice activities, which they learn and apply to complete the task successfully. All of the material is available to learners at precisely the moments they are primed to learn—at the points of trial and error.

For example, to boost profitability and respond to change more quickly, Siemens' global workforce had to learn to speak a common financial language. The company used a 48-hour simulation experience designed for 10,000 finance and business professionals. With a combination of technology and group-based activities, they simulated the challenge of growing a single-product company focused on the domestic market into a global industrial organization facing complex business decisions. The exercises allowed participants to practice the roles of financial analyst, finance manager, and project controller. In business review meetings, they worked in teams to complete a case study, drawing on expertise gained in previous simulation activities. The result: staff came away from the simulation with both a more deeply engrained understanding of the pressing need for a common language and a more robust grip on the language itself.

Reprint U0490C

About the Contributors

Paul Michelman is editor of *Harvard Management Update*.

Cassandra A. Frangos is HR practice leader at the Balanced Scorecard Collaborative.

Edward Prewitt is a contributor to *Harvard Management Update*.

Loren Gary is editor of newsletters at Harvard Business School Publishing.

Angelia Herrin is group editor of newsletters and conferences at Harvard Business School Publishing.

Martha Craumer is a business and marketing writer who lives in Cambridge, MA.

Alan Randolph is a consultant and business professor at the University of Baltimore. He is coauthor (with Ken Blanchard and John P. Carlos) of *Empowerment Takes More Than a Minute* and *The 3 Keys to Empowerment*.

Marie Gendron is a contributor to *Harvard Management Update*.

Kristen B. Donahue is a contributor to *Harvard Management Update*.

Alan G. Robinson is coauthor of *Ideas Are Free*.

Melissa Raffoni specializes in organizational development and executive coaching and is also a lecturer at the MIT Sloan School of Management.

David Boath is a partner in Accenture's Health & Sciences practice.

David Y. Smith is a partner at Accenture Learning.

Harvard Business Review Paperback Series

The Harvard Business Review Paperback Series offers the best thinking on cutting-edge management ideas from the world's leading thinkers, researchers, and managers. Designed for leaders who believe in the power of ideas to change business, these books will be useful to managers at all levels of experience, but especially senior executives and general managers. In addition, this series is widely used in training and executive development programs.

These books are priced at US$19.95
Price subject to change.

Title	Product #
Harvard Business Review **Interviews with CEOs**	3294
Harvard Business Review on **Advances in Strategy**	8032
Harvard Business Review on **Appraising Employee Performance**	7685
Harvard Business Review on **Becoming a High Performance Manager**	1296
Harvard Business Review on **Brand Management**	1445
Harvard Business Review on **Breakthrough Leadership**	8059
Harvard Business Review on **Breakthrough Thinking**	181X
Harvard Business Review on **Building Personal and Organizational Resilience**	2721
Harvard Business Review on **Business and the Environment**	2336
Harvard Business Review on **The Business Value of IT**	9121
Harvard Business Review on **Change**	8842
Harvard Business Review on **Compensation**	701X
Harvard Business Review on **Corporate Ethics**	273X
Harvard Business Review on **Corporate Governance**	2379
Harvard Business Review on **Corporate Responsibility**	2748
Harvard Business Review on **Corporate Strategy**	1429
Harvard Business Review on **Crisis Management**	2352
Harvard Business Review on **Culture and Change**	8369
Harvard Business Review on **Customer Relationship Management**	6994
Harvard Business Review on **Decision Making**	5572

Title	Product #
Harvard Business Review on **Developing Leaders**	5003
Harvard Business Review on **Doing Business in China**	6387
Harvard Business Review on **Effective Communication**	1437
Harvard Business Review on **Entrepreneurship**	9105
Harvard Business Review on **Finding and Keeping the Best People**	5564
Harvard Business Review on **Innovation**	6145
Harvard Business Review on **The Innovative Enterprise**	130X
Harvard Business Review on **Knowledge Management**	8818
Harvard Business Review on **Leadership**	8834
Harvard Business Review on **Leadership at the Top**	2756
Harvard Business Review on **Leadership in a Changed World**	5011
Harvard Business Review on **Leading in Turbulent Times**	1806
Harvard Business Review on **Managing Diversity**	7001
Harvard Business Review on **Managing High-Tech Industries**	1828
Harvard Business Review on **Managing People**	9075
Harvard Business Review on **Managing Projects**	6395
Harvard Business Review on **Managing the Value Chain**	2344
Harvard Business Review on **Managing Uncertainty**	9083
Harvard Business Review on **Managing Your Career**	1318
Harvard Business Review on **Marketing**	8040
Harvard Business Review on **Measuring Corporate Performance**	8826
Harvard Business Review on **Mergers and Acquisitions**	5556
Harvard Business Review on **Mind of the Leader**	6409
Harvard Business Review on **Motivating People**	1326
Harvard Business Review on **Negotiation**	2360
Harvard Business Review on **Nonprofits**	9091
Harvard Business Review on **Organizational Learning**	6153
Harvard Business Review on **Strategic Alliances**	1334
Harvard Business Review on **Strategies for Growth**	8850
Harvard Business Review on **Teams That Succeed**	502X
Harvard Business Review on **Turnarounds**	6366
Harvard Business Review on **What Makes a Leader**	6374
Harvard Business Review on **Work and Life Balance**	3286

Harvard Business Essentials

In the fast-paced world of business today, everyone needs a personal resource—a place to go for advice, coaching, background information, or answers. The Harvard Business Essentials series fits the bill. Concise and straightforward, these books provide highly practical advice for readers at all levels of experience. Whether you are a new manager interested in expanding your skills or an experienced executive looking to stay on top, these solution-oriented books give you the reliable tips and tools you need to improve your performance and get the job done. Harvard Business Essentials titles will quickly become your constant companions and trusted guides.

These books are priced at US$19.95, except as noted.
Price subject to change.

Title	Product #
Harvard Business Essentials: **Negotiation**	1113
Harvard Business Essentials: **Managing Creativity and Innovation**	1121
Harvard Business Essentials: **Managing Change and Transition**	8741
Harvard Business Essentials: **Hiring and Keeping the Best People**	875X
Harvard Business Essentials: **Finance for Managers**	8768
Harvard Business Essentials: **Business Communication**	113X
Harvard Business Essentials: **Manager's Toolkit ($24.95)**	2896
Harvard Business Essentials: **Managing Projects Large and Small**	3213
Harvard Business Essentials: **Creating Teams with an Edge**	290X
Harvard Business Essentials: **Entrepreneur's Toolkit**	4368
Harvard Business Essentials: **Coaching and Mentoring**	435X
Harvard Business Essentials: **Crisis Management**	4376
Harvard Business Essentials: **Time Management**	6336
Harvard Business Essentials: **Power, Influence, and Persuasion**	631X
Harvard Business Essentials: **Strategy**	6328

To order, call 1-800-668-6780, or go online at www.HBSPress.org

The Results-Driven Manager

The Results-Driven Manager series collects timely articles from Harvard Management Update and Harvard Management Communication Letter to help senior to middle managers sharpen their skills, increase their effectiveness, and gain a competitive edge. Presented in a concise, accessible format to save managers valuable time, these books offer authoritative insights and techniques for improving job performance and achieving immediate results.

These books are priced at US$14.95
Price subject to change.

Title	Product #
The Results-Driven Manager:	
Face-to-Face Communications for Clarity and Impact	3477
The Results-Driven Manager:	
Managing Yourself for the Career You Want	3469
The Results-Driven Manager:	
Presentations That Persuade and Motivate	3493
The Results-Driven Manager: **Teams That Click**	3507
The Results-Driven Manager:	
Winning Negotiations That Preserve Relationships	3485
The Results-Driven Manager: **Dealing with Difficult People**	6344
The Results-Driven Manager: **Taking Control of Your Time**	6352
The Results-Driven Manager: **Getting People on Board**	6360
The Results-Driven Manager:	
Motivating People for Improved Performance	7790
The Results-Driven Manager: **Becoming an Effective Leader**	7804
The Results-Driven Manager:	
Managing Change to Reduce Resistance	7812
The Results-Driven Manager:	
Hiring Smart for Competitive Advantage	9726
The Results-Driven Manager: **Retaining Your Best People**	9734
The Results-Driven Manager:	
Business Etiquette for the New Workplace	9742

Management Dilemmas: Case Studies from the Pages of Harvard Business Review

When facing a difficult management challenge, wouldn't it be great if you could turn to a panel of experts to help guide you to the right decision? Now you can, with books from the Management Dilemmas series. Drawn from the pages of Harvard Business Review, each insightful guide poses a range of familiar and perplexing business situations and shares the wisdom of a small group of leading experts on how each of them would resolve the problem. Engagingly written, these interactive, solutions-oriented collections allow readers to match wits with the experts. They are designed to help managers hone their instincts and problem-solving skills to make sound judgment calls on everyday management dilemmas.

These books are priced at US$19.95
Price subject to change.

Title	Product #
Management Dilemmas: **When Change Comes Undone**	5038
Management Dilemmas: **When Good People Behave Badly**	5046
Management Dilemmas: **When Marketing Becomes a Minefield**	290X
Management Dilemmas: **When People Are the Problem**	7138
Management Dilemmas: **When Your Strategy Stalls**	712X

How to Order

Harvard Business School Press publications are available worldwide
from your local bookseller or online retailer.
You can also call

1-800-668-6780

Our product consultants are available to help you
8:00 a.m.–6:00 p.m., Monday–Friday, Eastern Time.
Outside the U.S. and Canada, call: 617-783-7450
Please call about special discounts for quantities greater than ten.

You can order online at

www.HBSPress.org